TRUST THE
Curves

by
JANIECE RENDON

Copyright © 2016 by Janiece Rendon
All content is copyright 2016 by Janiece Rendon, Janiece Rendon International, LLC

All rights reserved worldwide.

No part of this book may be reproduced, redistributed, transmitted, retransmitted, translated, sold, given away, decompiled or otherwise circumvented by any means, electronic or mechanical, including photocopying, recording, or by any information storage or retrieval system, without written permission from the publisher, Manifest Publishing.

Warning and disclaimer: While author and publisher have made every effort to provide accurate information, publisher cannot control author websites or third-party websites and assumes no responsibility.

This book is designed to provide information and processes used by Janiece Rendon. Every effort has been made to make it as complete and accurate as possible, but no warranty is implied.

The information in this book is provided on an "as is" basis. Janiece Rendon International, LLC, and the author make no guarantees that you will experience the same results as the author. The author and Janiece Rendon International, LLC also have no responsibility to any person or entity with respect to loss or damage arising from information contained in this book or from any programs or document that may accompany it.

For privacy, some names have been changed.

ISBN-13:978-1944913007 (Manifest Publishing)
ISBN-10:1944913009

PRAISE FOR JANIECE RENDON

"Finally, a book that tells it like it is. Janiece is amazing in going from unemployed with no high school diploma to receiving not one, but TWO Master's Degrees. 'Resilient' doesn't even begin to describe the tenacity of Janiece Rendon. She has an amazing ability to kick bad luck right in the face, and come out shining on the other side."

~ Tonja Waring
The Manifesting Mindset

"Janiece, thank you for your words of encouragement and your guidance, I really appreciated the feedback and your positive attitude! You will be missed around here!"

~ Tina Gustafson,
MillerCoors Brewing Maintenance
Senior Specialist

Janiece is a wonderful, thoughtful person who truly takes the time to listen to people and offer her encouragement and support. She can be counted on to have a bit of wisdom to share with everyone. Thank you again and I wish you well in your new opportunities!

~ Melissa Kuhn
MillerCoors Brewing Company

Janiece is always ready to help people and always has a smile to share. People feel good in her presence.

~ Linda Rhea

"If you've ever thought, 'If only I knew then what I know now,' this book is for you. Through her personal stories and life lessons, Janiece Rendon shares strategies for living a more meaningful life and stepping into your greatness."

~ Michelle Prince
Ziglar Certified Speaker /
America's Productivity Coach
Best-Selling Author & Self Publishing Expert

"When first starting Janiece's book, I was compelled to travel back to my own childhood. The book is written with Janiece's stories and then her life lessons, allowing the reader to not only enjoy her stories but to also allow us as a reader to simultaneously remember our journey. This made me feel happy."

~ Suzi Nelson
Executive Director Countries and CrossRoads

"Janiece has a compelling story of triumphing over every curve in her life. Her memoir is written from the heart, like everything else she does. Her passion is to provide you or someone you know with the same hope that she used back then to be happy and thriving today. Only get her book if you want to get past the curves in your life!"

~ Deana Bossio

"Janiece Rendon is a beautiful human being with much to give. Her humor, compassion and innate sense of integrity shine through in all her communications. She is a wonderful teacher, coach and personal cheerleader. I highly recommend any program Janiece has to offer as I know it will be fantastic!"

> ~ **Debby Stinson**
> **Marketing & PR Manager at**
> **Museum of Art/Washington State University**

"You know that song called "This Little Light of Mine"? Well I am convinced it was written about Janiece. This lady absolutely glows from within! She is always singing and smiling - lighting up the room with Christ's love!

> ~ **Cay Barrett**
> **Senior Risk Management Analyst at Molson**
> **Coors Brewing Company**

"I have been friends with Janiece for 17 years, during that time I have watched her shine light into darkness, she stood up to her family when her nieces were being abused and brought them into her home to be her daughters. She stood tall and set her face like a flint to keep them safe and to give them a loving home. She was rejected and scorned but persevered for them. She has brought so much joy into my life, and taught me about forgiveness and compassion through her testimony. I love and admire the woman that she is how she steps out of her comfort zone to speak the truth in love and this has helped me to also step out. Thank you Janiece."

> ~ **Cindy Schneider**
> **MillerCoors Brewing Company**

"Janiece Rendon is a breath of fresh air. Not afraid to try something new or find a unique perspective, Janiece is a committed, loving, positive source of encouragement for her family, friends, and soon-to-be friends (because if you need a friend, Janiece is there, she is a lover of people). She takes the lead by setting goals and making them happen, and builds others up with her words, photographs, and support. She is a true blessing to those of us fortunate enough to know her.

~ **Wendy Lawson**
Gold Ambassador, Plexus Worldwide

"Janiece Rendon is one of the most, teachable, coachable professionals I have ever had the privilege and honor of working with. She is willing to do the work and go the extra mile so she can help those who are placed in her life. Her book will change your world and create a dynamic that will take you to where you were created to be. Janiece is real. She is ready to take you to the next level.

~ **Beatrice Bruno**
The Drill Sergeant of Life

IN LOVING MEMORY

My Mother, Evelyn Gurule
Thank you for taking the step into wanting
more from life and moving to the suburbs
to give me a better life.
Thank you for always believing in me and giving me
the stability to follow my dreams, which lead me to the
path of greatness.

My Father, Dave Gurule
Thank you for wanting more for your life.
It has been a pleasure getting to know you and
your family in the last 15 or so years.

TABLE OF CONTENTS

Where Do I Belong?....................................1
My Proud Mother.......................................7
The Brady Bunch.......................................10
Failed Entrepreneurship............................14
Are You Going to Find a Real Job? 17
Getting Serious About My Life 20
Determined to Succeed............................25
No Matter What 25
Finding God in Corporate 32
The Tease "Lead Position".........................36
The Power of Determination....................39
Rock Bottom 47
Facing the Giant..53
The Power to Ask for More 58
Attitude is Everything 62
The Power of Tenacity..............................66
My Soul Mate Finds Me 71
Like the Whole World...............................75
The Gift of Forgiveness.............................84
I Am Strong 87
The Proposal 90
The Gift of Life from Our Donor 96
Thanksgiving Wedding 102
Learning to Ride a Motorcycle 105
Ask for What You Want..........................112

ACKNOWLEDGEMENTS

I want to thank God, for loving me and being by my side through all the uncertainty in my life.

My loving husband, Joe Rendon, and children, Adrianna Rendon, and Cherrelle Vigil. Thank you for all the support and love you shared with me on this road to fulfill my dream and passion. Joe, thank you for letting me share my dream in the beginning of our relationship. You have supported me and believed in me each and every day. Adrianna thank you for calling me Mom and believing in me. You listened to my presentations many nights with support and love.

My coach, Gary Barnes, who without his love, encouragement and insight, I would not be where I am today. Thank you.

My publisher, Tonja Waring, thank you for being the light in so many people's lives to help us shine you are more than a publisher, you are an amazing friend who always believed in me and encouraged me through the process to become an author.

Anita Beck, thank you for proofreading the words to let them flow.

Faith Armour, thank you for seeing something in me that I did not see in myself. You gave me the spark to ignite my fire, taught me that I could get an education, and taught me how to build relationships.

The late Zig Ziglar, thank you for inspiring so many people in your life (especially me) with your signature message, "You can have everything in life you want if you will just help enough other people get what they want."

Marilyn Peterson, thank you for the introduction to Zig Ziglar on audio-cassette one night working graveyard. You had the courage to speak up and risk rejection.

Beatrice Bruno, "The Drill Sergeant of Life," thank you for helping me step out of fear into Greatness.

Sharlene Douthit, "Financially Fit Females," thank you for setting me on my journey to entrepreneurship.

Debbie Davis, thank you for sharing your faith and bringing my mother and me to the Lord. And, for believing in me for more than 20 years. You called me the next Oprah and that meant the world to me.

Diane Ban, thank you for the great opportunity to see how internally strong I really was. It is a pleasure to call you friend.

Don Rust, thank you for believing in me and sharing your knowledge of life.

Bob, thank you for sharing the idea to write a proposal to get my high school diploma.

Joe Wiggins, thank you for pushing me to remember names and for planting the seed of Toastmasters International.

And, thank you to the many others who touched my life and helped me to become the person I am today.

JANIECE RENDON

Janiece Rendon is a woman filled with tenacity, passion and heart. Laid off five times in 31 years from the same Fortune 500 company, she learned what she calls the F.A.C.T.S. of Life (Forgiveness, Attitude, Choice, Trust and Step into Your Greatness.) These simple F.A.C.T. S. kept her in the game and thriving through her many moments of uncertainty.

Janiece began her career in production without a high school diploma. Inspired by the teachings of Zig Ziglar, she was determined to take advantage of the educational opportunities she never had growing up. Not only did she graduate from her high school at 34 years old, she went on to earn a Bachelor of Science degree in Business Administration: Human Resource Management, and later graduated with a dual Master of Arts degree in Communication and Psychology.

Today she is an Adjunct Professor of Public Speaking at Colorado Heights University. She inspires others through her keynotes, trainings and private coaching. She lives in Denver, Colorado with her husband and daughter, is an avid photographer, and makes daily Facebook posts on her journey of "Walking with Janiece."

FOREWORD

How many times have you had things go against you? How many times have you given up? Each of us has faced adversity at one time or another. Each of us have had to find our strength to move forward. Janiece has an incredible fortitude for working her way out of adversity and making the best of a bad situation.

Janiece Rendon demonstrates perfectly how we can rise up from nearly impossible circumstances and still manage to get exactly what we want out of life. Although her grit and determination is enveloped in a sweet, sunshiny bundle of possibility, make no mistake about it, Janiece is relentless in her pursuit of creating her life the way she wants it.

A great example was Janiece's ability to get her high school diploma (not her G.E.D.) when she was 34 years old! Janiece wanted to attend college and realized she needed her high school diploma, which she didn't have. (She had more than enough credits to graduate, however she was missing one-half credit in physical education so they wouldn't give her a diploma.)

They told her there was nothing they could do for her. She was too old to go to high school. They told her she could get a G.E.D.

Well, Janiece believed she deserved her high school diploma, and she was not going to take no for an answer. She was too old to go back to high school, so she wrote a proposal with a plan to get the ½ credit required! She logged in all her hours at the gym, and then had the gym sign off on it. When she went to the school board with the hours she had been working out, they accepted it for her ½ credit, and she received her high school diploma!

If you want to achieve more that what seems likely where you are today, then remember Janiece's

F.A.C.T.S. OF LIFE

Forgiveness, Attitude, Choice, Trust, and Step into your Greatness

Or better yet, call Janiece. Of the many people I have worked with through the years, she has inspired me the most. She is quick to get things done and always willing to do what it takes, regardless of her circumstances. I guarantee she will teach you and inspire you to move beyond <u>anything</u> that has stopped you from living your dream.

Go on! Live your best life!

Tonja Waring
Top 3 Infomercial Host in 2012
Sold Over $50MM on TV
www.TonjaWaring.com

CHAPTER 1

Where Do I Belong?

> "Success is a zigzag line of trials and errors. The first time I spoke in front of people, I cried through the whole speech. Worst part about it? I invited all my friends and coworkers. I packed the house. I survived, and they still believe in me. I now know I belong behind the mic encouraging others."
>
> ~Janiece Rendon

I was born an unattractive, dark-skinned, overweight Hispanic girl who came from a family of alcoholics and drug addicts.

I don't remember ever feeling like I belonged; not just with my family, either. I never belonged anywhere. I wanted to be "cool" like my family, but I was too afraid of drugs to ever try them. However, that didn't keep me from trying to fit in other ways.

One time, I went to a party with my aunt who was close in age to me. When I walked into the kitchen, I was shocked to find them sitting at the kitchen table with needles hanging out of their arms. I was even more shocked when I looked up and realized one of those arms belonged to my aunt.

Heroin.

Besides alcohol, heroin was the drug of choice in my family and in the neighborhood. Another time when I was out with my aunt, there was a drive by shooting. And then, there was the time I was hanging out with the wrong crowd in a park, and before I knew it, the police were surrounding us with rifles. I can remember it like it was yesterday; the people tried to scatter, the sounds of the leaves crunching around me. It was as if I was in a slow-motion movie, but it was very real. The police asked for our ID's and said if anything happened to the others, we would get called in for questioning. I was scared to death.

All I wanted was to be cool. I thought if I at least hung out with the cool people, I would be cool, and I was not even good at that.

* * * * *

I was born in 1960 to Evelyn and Dave Gurule in a small town called, Raton, New Mexico. Shortly thereafter, we moved to Northglenn, Colorado which was about 14 miles from Denver. We lived there until my senior year in high school. My father was a white-collar employee and was embarrassed that my mother worked on a production line catching cookies at a major bakery in Denver. He told her not to say anything about her job to his friends.

No surprise that my parents divorced when I was only four years old. I didn't have much to do with my father after that.

I was my mother's only child, and I lived with her. She would sometimes take me to the bakery and show me off to her co-workers. It was fun meeting all of her friends. The bakery smelled like my mother. Or, shall I say, my mother smelled like the bakery. Her clothes always smelled like glazed donuts.

My mother was a hard worker and the sole breadwinner of our family. She had to pay the mortgage and support me, so she worked nights while I was young. Even though she graduated from high school, she could barely read or write.

No one in my family went to college.

* * * * *

I had many babysitters over the years. I was so shy and would cry for hours when I wasn't with my mother. I missed her so much when she was gone. You can imagine that my mother had a hard time finding sitters for me.

When I was seven or eight years old, the husband of my babysitter walked into the kitchen naked during the middle of the night while I was sleeping on the couch. I told my mother what happened and what I had seen. She began searching for another sitter immediately.

Another time when I was around 10 years old, my babysitter was trying to get me to stop crying so she had me smoke a cigarette. That didn't work. So, she told my mother that she could not watch me any longer.

Eventually, Mom found Emily, our next-door neighbor. She had a daycare and was my babysitter for as long as I can remember. My mom used to tease me and say that Emily was my second mom. In many ways, she was.

Emily was married to Dean, and they had an only child, Bobby. Bobby and I got along very well. We were the oldest of all the babysitting kids whom Emily watched. We loved to entertain them! Bobby loved Red Skelton so he would imitate him. I, on the other hand, loved to dance and sing. We had a captive audience, and they would sit there and let us perform for them. It was so much fun.

Then, one by one, their parents would pick them up at the end of the day, and our captive audience would slowly disappear. When Bobby had to get ready for bed so he could get up for school in the morning, I would sit there waiting for my mom to pick me up, which was around midnight. While I waited, Dean would sit in his favorite chair smoking a pipe and reading the paper. Occasionally, he would glance up over the paper to see what I was doing. More often than not, I would be sitting on the couch, staring at the door, waiting and wishing for my mom to come.

A car would drive by, and I would jump up and say, "Is that my mom?" It never was.

Eventually Dean would say, "Okay, it is time to close the door now. It is getting late."

I would ask, "Can we leave it open until one more car comes by? I know it will be my mom."

He would say, "Okay, we can keep it cracked just a little bit, for a little while longer."

That was very nice of him to keep the door cracked open for me when he knew my mom was not going to be home anytime soon.

I feel like I was always waiting for my mom to come pick me up and take me home. Although I had some great times at the babysitter's, I wanted to be in my own home with my mom. I was always the last child to be picked up.

Emily was a great baker. She made homemade breads, cookies, and lots of other good stuff. One time, I wanted to cook for her, so I went and bought everything I needed to make homemade tortillas. I mixed up the masa and rolled out the dough. I put it on the stove, but something went terribly wrong!

I threw that tortilla away, and told her that the next one would be better. Oh, no! The next one turned out the same as the first. It was yellow and did not roll like my mother's tortillas. I couldn't figure out what I did wrong. I felt so bad.

Later, I discovered I had bought the wrong tortilla mix. I bought mix for corn tortillas instead of flour tortillas. Emily told me it was fine, and she appreciated me for trying to do something nice for her.

Janiece's Life's Lessons

➤ Little things done with the right attitude make a big difference.

➤ When someone does something special for you, even if it is a flop, appreciate the gesture.

CHAPTER 2

My Proud Mother

> "Two of the many things that my mom taught me were to pay back what you borrow, and do more than expected."
> ~Janiece Rendon

My mother moved me out of the city to the suburbs because she wanted a better life for us. She didn't want to be like her brothers, sister or parents. And, she certainly didn't want me to be like that. There were not a lot of single women raising children by themselves then, let alone women like my mom who owned her own home. Emily would often tell Dean, "You had better behave! If Evelyn can make it by herself, so can I." I was always proud of my mom and wanted to be like her.

One time, my mother was talking about how she could not make the house payment. She asked her brother for a loan. His wife was not too thrilled with the idea and made a big stink about it. How could they treat her like that? My mother raised her brothers and sister while their parents were in the bar. You would think at the very least that they could help her out when she needed the help. It hurt her deeply. My mom said she would never ask for help again.

From what I witnessed growing up, my mother was always helping others and not getting much of anything in return. I saw many people take advantage of her. At one point in her life, she was not able to buy a washer or dryer, because her credit was ruined after she cosigned on a loan with one of her brothers or sister, and guess what? They didn't repay the loan.

I was amazed at my mother and how she became so independent. I became a lot like her in many ways. I do not like to ask for help, do not know how to ask for help, and many times I have allowed people to take advantage of me.

There is a difference between helping people and enabling people. My mother enabled people to stay where they were. She did it out of kindness and love. She couldn't see that they were not going to change. After I became an adult, I would tell her, "Do NOT sacrifice your credit to help others who are not willing to help themselves."

Mom was a smart woman, however, she couldn't seem to let go of her need to care for her siblings. I later found out her need to enable her family was also the reason my dad didn't want to stay with her. He wanted more for his life and felt like her family was going to drag him down, too. Unfortunately, she just couldn't let go of them. So, he made the decision to leave.

In her passing, these people continued in life without her. It makes me upset that the sacrifices she made for them did not make an impact on them to change their lives.

Janiece's Life's Lessons

➤ Your credit is important.

➤ It is okay to ask for help. (We cannot do life alone.)

➤ It is okay to help people. However, teach them to help themselves live independently. Do not teach them to be dependent upon you.

➤ It is okay to leave some people behind in order for you to move forward in life.

➤ The best way to be remembered is to teach people to fish.

➤ Do not do business with friends and family.

CHAPTER 3

The Brady Bunch

> "Remove those darkened lenses of abuse and replace them with God's lenses of forgiveness and be free."
>
> ~Janiece Rendon

My mother met a man, Ben, who had five children; four girls and one boy. All of them moved in with us except the oldest daughter. To me, it felt like our house had been invaded by aliens! As I said before, I was very shy and insecure. This situation did not help at all.

My new sisters were very pretty. One of them won a beauty pageant from a church in Denver. My brother looked like Donny Osmond and all the girls loved him. I, on the other hand, was awkward, overweight, and my hair was as unmanageable as a Brillo pad. One day, I overheard my step dad telling my mom to do something with "her" hair… meaning my hair. Ouch. I wanted to be pretty and cool like my sisters were; however, that was not happening.

The kids were all older than I was and in their own little clique. I felt left out. Even though we lived in the same house, they went to different schools than I did. It would have been nice to go to school together as a family, but of course, they wanted to stay at the school they were in and so did I.

They did not like my mom's rules. My mother expected us to do things like go to school and behave. So, the girls moved out as soon as they could. I do not remember if they graduated from high school or not. The oldest girl, Laverne, was very independent and had her own place already. The second oldest, Brenda, loved to dance. One time, she had a party and got in big trouble. Boy, was my mother upset.

The youngest sister, Lorraine, and I were the "lucky" ones; we had dish duty. Velma, the third oldest loved to cook. When she cooked, she used every pan and dish in the house. It seemed like Lorraine and I would wash dishes for hours.

The youngest of the bunch was the boy, Joey. He was a year older than I was, and we got along pretty well... until we were the last ones left in the house, and then we fought quite a bit. He would leave me home alone, and before he would walk out the door, he would always say, "Someone's watching you." Being the fraidy cat that I was, I would sit in the kitchen where I could see both the front and back door at the same time until our parents came home.

Joey and I would fight about our parents and our parents would fight about us. In reality, it is too bad we had to fight at all. I remember one time my mom and stepdad were fighting, and I had had enough. I went into their room to my stepdad's side of the bed and with one dramatic sweep, cleared off everything on the nightstand with my arm not really thinking. The drinking glass that was there, broke and sliced my wrist very badly.

I immediately went to the kitchen where they were fighting. I was crying and my mom rushed me to the hospital to get stitches. They kept asking me if I was trying to commit suicide. I said, "No, that is really dumb. I was upset, so I cleared Ben's nightstand with my arm, and cut my wrist."

I never did anything like that again. Not only did it hurt, but my mom chewed me out. All the way to the hospital she kept saying, "What were you thinking? Blah blah blah."

My brother moved out after high school. It was a two-edge sword, I missed him, yet I was glad he was gone.

It wasn't all bad. I do have some great memories of my time with my sisters and brother. They loved music as well as I did, so we kind of connected with music. And, we would go to Juarez, Mexico as a family almost every year and have a blast. One time we forgot the youngest daughter at the store, and we had to go back for her.

Janiece's Life's Lessons

- If you don't like to wash dishes, then learn to cook; or learn something, anything, that you would like to do. You can do it!

- If you are going to do something to interrupt a bad situation (like break up an argument), make sure you be productive, not make it worse.

- When you have a large family going on a trip (or you are part of a team) be sure to make sure everyone is present before you get back on the road. Take care of each other.

- Remember the good times, and reflect on those good times. You can rewrite the story of your past.

CHAPTER 4

Failed Entrepreneurship

> "Take responsibility for failures and accomplishments of the past and present in order to move on to exciting new adventures."
> ~Janiece Rendon

My stepfather bought his grandmother's house in Denver. My parents fixed it up and moved it to a new lot. It was official, we were moving from Northglenn too Denver. I would have to leave all my friends and move so far away…

You see, I was so shy that moving to Denver seemed like a million miles away, even though it was only a few miles south. I had no friends in Denver and did not want to move, so I stayed at the Northglenn house cleaning until the day before they rented it. It was the perfect move for my parents because their jobs were right down the street.

I, on the other hand, had a tough time with even the thought of moving. I wondered how I would meet anyone, because I was no longer in high school. I began working at a convenience store close to the house. That job helped me meet new friends.

One day my stepdad said, "We should open up a barbershop." He had always wanted a barbershop, and he wanted me to run it. I had taken Cosmetology in high school.

I said, "Okay."

My parents put up the money for the shop, and I was going to manage the business. I was very immature so my first adventure as an entrepreneur was a complete disaster. It was a great location right on the corner of 38th and Federal in North Denver. I named it, "The Hair to be Looking Sharp." At the time, I thought it was a great name. I hired a couple of people, and it was fine for awhile. However, it did not work out long term. I did not take it seriously and did not have the business skills to run the shop successfully. My step-dad closed the shop and sold all the equipment. I was back to looking for a job.

I worked at a few barbershops, 7-11, UtoteM, fast food places, cleaning offices, you name it, I probably did it. Finally, I ended up cutting hair in a very popular barbershop in West Denver, called Avondale Barbers.

Janiece's Life's Lessons

➢ You will thrive. Give yourself time and everything will be okay.

➢ When moving to a new location, working where a lot of people come and go, you will eventually make friends.

➢ When life gives you an opportunity; take it seriously and learn as much as you can.

➢ When someone is backing you up with finances be sure to be grateful; work hard to be successful, and appreciate those who have helped you along the way.

CHAPTER 5

Are You Going to Find a Real Job?

> "There are a world of opportunities waiting for you, pick one and go for it!"
> ~ Janiece Rendon

My mom kept asking me, "Janiece when are you going to find a real job?"

I said, "Mom, I am going to find all the jobs I don't like until I find the one I do." I was so naïve. I kept thinking about what my mom kept telling me, "Find a job with benefits and a pension." So finally, a coworker and I decided to look for new jobs. We began looking in the newspaper (That is how you found a job back then.)

I said, "How about this one?" then hesitated. "It says you need a 'rezoom'."

He laughed at me and said, "It is a 'res-oo-may' (resume); a piece of paper which tells them what you have done." We laughed at my naivety and kept looking for a job. I liked where I worked. It was a great barbershop, but it did not have benefits and a retirement plan. My mom was on me all the time about finding a job with benefits.

I applied for a job at a student loan place because they had good benefits. I was excited for the interview. However, during the interview, the woman said, "You will never get a job with this company. You cannot read or write," and then, she threw my application back at me. I was devastated.

Well, it didn't matter how cruel she was, my friend and I did get jobs there. We began as temporaries, putting together loan payment books. I eventually applied for a job as a skiptracer (someone who finds people who skip out on their loans) and was hired fulltime with benefits. It was a fun job. I called people all day trying to locate those who weren't paying their student loans. I often thought about that woman telling me I would never get a job there, and thought to myself, "Well, I showed her. I am working for this company." I worked there for about a year.

At that time, I was a partier and did not have a care in the world and certainly didn't think about my career. I called in sick all the time. Then one day, I called in sick, but this time I told my boss that I would have to quit. I was not sick; I stayed up partying all night and wanted to sleep. As soon as I hung up the phone, I knew I had made the biggest mistake of my life.

I realized how dumb that was and knew my mom was going to get mad at me for quitting a good job. There was nothing my mom was going to tell me that I was not already telling myself. Here I go again looking for a job.

Janiece's Life Lessons

- Figure out early in life what you want to do when you grow up; then go for it!

- Learn new words to add to your vocabulary. This way you do not look ignorant in sounding out words in front of people.

- There will be times in life when someone will tell you something about yourself that is harsh. Whether it is true or not, you do not need to carry their words with you for the rest of your life. Let it go…

- Do not believe what people tell you. You can do anything you put your mind to.

- Do not quit a job unless you have another one lined up.

- You know you are growing up when there is nothing your parents are going to tell you that you are not already telling yourself.

CHAPTER 6

Getting Serious About My Life

> "Reach your hand out to life, and life will you give you multitudes of blessings."
> ~Janiece Rendon

In 1985, I began a job (Or, should I say a journey?) that would last longer than any other job I had. This journey has taken me to many fabulous places, especially to my calling and finding God. I was in my mid-twenties and had so much to learn.

Little did I know, I was about to find many jobs within the same company; all of which have created a journey of empowerment and inner courage that have lead me to believe in myself. Now, I have been given the opportunity to help others believe in themselves. The greatest enjoyment in life I have found, is watching others step into their light and see the light bulb go on. There is something about watching someone look at themselves differently with pride and joy.

One day a friend of mine said, "Let's go apply at Coors and get a job there."

I said, "Why would we work there?" She said that there were some really good looking guys who worked there. Some real "babes" she called them! That was a good enough reason for me, so off we went.

We began working in production at the paper-packaging plant. I didn't know anything about working in a high-paced production line. The reason we chose this location was that it paid extra money for working in Boulder, Colorado.

I think it was around $.45 more an hour. We were the only two girls working there, and the men did not appreciate us in their workspace. My friend had long fingernails and one of the guys told her that she would not have those nails at the end of the shift. He was right! By the end of the day, all of her nails broke off from the fast movement of the paper and machines.

The paper itself was so large I had my arms open as far as I could and could barely load the machine. I was told not to let the paper get low because the machine would jam. When the machine goes down, it costs the company a lot of money. Thank goodness, I had a bandana because the sweat was dripping down my face so fast I could barely see.

My friend laughed at me. I told her that it would be her turn on this machine tomorrow, and we would see who would be laughing then. We did not last there very long before we went back to the temporary labor pool office and asked to be reassigned.

They assigned us to the end plant (another production job this time in Golden, Colorado). This job was fun and the guys we worked with were cool. They were making around $20 an hour, and we only were making around $2.35 an hour for the same work. My job was to load the lids of the cans into this long bag that would eventually meet up with the can and be filled with product. Not sure, how long we were in this position, but the assignment ran out.

Here we go again, back to the temporary labor pool office for another reassignment.

* * * * *

Our next assignment was to work at the glass plant. This was the perfect job for us! We broke bottles all day long. I am telling you, if I was frustrated with *anything* in life, this job was a major release of tension.

We had the perfect shift. We worked from 6:00 am until 2:00 pm. Everyday, there were stacks of pallets filled with bottles to break. We got so good at breaking bottles, we created a system to clear out all the pallets during our shift. Funny though, we never ran out of bottles for the next day. They hired a couple of other people, and we trained them.

Much to my surprise and without any warning, my friend and I were getting the boot. The boss called us in after our shift one day and told us we were no longer needed. He gave no explanation. We asked if there was something we had done wrong. He ignored us and told us to leave. And, we did not receive pay for our final day's work.

It didn't go unrecognized that we were the only two Hispanic girls. Of course, we did not think this was fair. Our friends and family began to tell us not to go work for this company, as they were prejudiced against Hispanics.

Yes, it was unfair that we were the only two who were laid off. Yes, it was unfair that he did not pay us for our final day. We did not have any proof of wrongdoing, or at least we were too naïve to know how to prove it. So, there was nothing we could do. What I now realize is that if we had won the battle and stayed working in that job, I would have missed out on what would lead to my future success.

"Sometimes, life has a way of leading you to your destiny."

~ Janiece Rendon

Just think, I could have broken bottles for 30 years and totally missed out on my destiny in life! Thank you, God, for the opportunity to let it go, and to move forward toward something greater than I could ever had imagined.

Janiece's Life Lessons

➢ You may feel you are going in circles not getting anywhere, but do not give up; your roadmap will get clear.

➢ Not every job you try will be the perfect fit; what if you have something better waiting for you in the future?

➢ It does not matter if the person working next to you makes more money, what matters is you keep striving to be better. The money will come.

➢ If you have the skills to set up a system to make things run smoother in one job; you can do it in most any job.

➢ Life is unfair at times; people make poor decisions that affect your life. Consider the possibility you were not meant to stay there.

➢ Sometimes being naïve will save you from fighting a battle that will lead you to winning the war.

CHAPTER 7

Determined to Succeed No Matter What

> "One thing I'm very certain of is our experiences in life connect together. I believe there is a reason for everything."
> ~Janiece Rendon

Back to the temporary labor pool office we go where the only production jobs they had were in the main plant. The only problem for me was that you had to ride this thing called a "man-lift" to get from the production line to the lunchroom. A man-lift was a rubber band type of elevator that I had to get on to take me from one floor to another. I am scared of heights, so this was a stretch for me.

Looking up or down, I could literally see the floor below or the floor above me. My stomach would lurch. I would have to ride from a huge hole in the basement to the top floor. If anyone missed their step, he could fall and hurt himself very badly. Before I would be able to ride the man-lift, I would have to be certified. I went through the man-lift training. I was going to conquer my fear; I was going to ride this rubber band thing. Well, I mastered riding it up to the floor above me. However, I could not get it into my head that I had to step up to go down. Long story short, I did not complete my certification to ride the man-lift. So off to the temporary labor pool office for yet another reassignment. I think they now knew me by my first name.

* * * * *

Fortunately, the temporary labor pool was out of production jobs. The only thing they had for us were office jobs. My friend took a temporary job as a secretary. I did not know how to type. The woman told me that I had to be able to type in order to get an office job. I told her that I did not know how to type very well, but that I was an expert when it comes to 10-key skills.

Back when I was doing all kinds of odd jobs, I decided I wanted a job counting the inventory for stores. You had to wear the calculator on your hip, which meant you had to know 10-key by touch. I wanted this job so bad that I taught myself how to 10-key by touch with a phone while I held it on my hip. The 10-key pad and the numbers on the phone were the exact opposite.

I practiced every night until I learned how to do it without looking, and I became lightning fast. One thing was true, I had tenacity. I was determined to get that job, and I did.

Who knew this menial job was going to help me in the future to get a job in the office of a major corporation?

The woman was not too thrilled with my lack of typing skills, however, she said there was a job in Microfilm if I wanted to take it. I would get paid production wages because I could not type. I did not care. I needed a job. I had just taken custody of my aunt's two children - two boys. One was two years old and the other was three. Both of their parents went to jail for a year, and I stepped up to raise them. I literally grew up overnight. I went from partying all the time to raising two kids. Later, I found out the youngest was deaf. I now had to learn a new language - sign language.

When I got this job in Microfilm, my attitude was completely different. I had the new attitude of, "I am going to prove myself for my next job. I am going to learn as much as I can for my next job. I am going to show up everyday and be on time." I was going to do whatever they needed me to do, so I could learn new skills for my next job. I was going to be a sponge and take in everything I could. And, that's what I did.

One time my car broke down, and I had to take a cab to work (Well, I chose to take a cab to work.) That cab ride cost me more than I was going make the entire day. It didn't matter. I was more committed to showing up on time, even if it wasn't easy or cost me more than I made. Sometimes, you have to do what is necessary to achieve success. Success for me at that time was a good work record.

As Faith Would Guide Me

This position entailed filming documents through this huge machine for recordkeeping on film. There were boxes and boxes of papers to film. I was excited because I could see by the sheer volume of boxes, I would have this job for a very long time. I have the tendency to find better ways of doing things. They would open a box, pull out a paper, pull out the staple, film one side of the paper, turn it over then film the other side then staple it back together and put it in the filmed box. I created a new system.

First, I prepped all the papers to be filmed. This way when you sit at the camera you do not have to stop, you can continually film. It was amazing how fast I could film the documents. As I was prepping some insurance documents, I ran across a document with the name of the boss at the glass plant who let us go. The insurance document had all his information on it, phone number and address. A quick thought ran through my head to go do something stupid. I wanted to. I really did. However, I am not that kind of person who gets even with revenge. My mother taught me that revenge would take care of itself. I ignored the impulse and let it go.

As I looked at the situation from a different point of view, he released me from a job of breaking bottles to an opportunity for an amazing life filled with education and a better road to following a dream worth living.

Faith was the name of my boss in Microfilm. A perfect fit for the beginning of my journey. She was my first mentor along this journey with corporate and life. In me, she saw potential. She treated me with respect. She changed the perspective of how I looked at myself.

> "My life began to change because I began to change."
> ~Janiece Rendon

One of the things she said was, "Nobody is better than you, they just have had different experiences in life, such as a college education, their parents had money, or they had different connections." She planted many seeds in my garden of life. All the while, she kept pouring water in the soil, which grew a new hope for my future and what I wanted to do.

We would walk to the other side of the building and people would say hello to her all the time. I thought to myself, "I want to know as many people as her." I got brave one day and asked, "How do you know so many people?"

She said, "I have been working here a long time and have built relationships along the way."

What a concept! I was going to do that, too, and before I knew it, I was on my way to making many connections and friends. She would tell me, "Janiece, no matter what you want to do in life, this company has a job for you to do it." She also said, "Take advantage of all the benefits the company has to offer you. Invest in the 401K savings plan. Another great benefit they have is tuition reimbursement; they pay for your college."

I wondered if she took advantage of the tuition reimbursement plan, but I never asked. I thought to myself, "Why should I do it if she did not do it? But, then, what does that matter? I can still do it even if she hasn't." Although, she planted the seeds in my ground of being, it was up to me to keep watering the soil until I blossomed.

Janiece's Life Lessons

- ➤ Step into your fear. It does not matter whether you master the fear; what matters is that you faced it.

- ➤ If they are asking for skills you do not have, let them know of the skills you do have and maybe they can use those skills instead.

- ➤ If you do not have a skill for a position you want, figure out how you can learn that skill; and then master it.

- ➤ When you have a purpose, your destiny will happen.

- Come up with a motto that will carry you through to success.

- Sometimes, you have to pay the price to keep your word to yourself.

- Look for opportunities to do things different.

- Your revenge will be short lived. The best revenge is bettering yourself; then letting your destiny fall in place.

- Find positive mentors in your journey of life.

- Keep pouring hope in your soil to grow a new life.

- Make connections wherever you go; you never know how they may change your direction in life.

CHAPTER 8

Finding God in Corporate

> "Give God your pain and he will turn it into your purpose."
> ~ Janiece Rendon

Eventually, I was running out of documents to film. Technology was changing, and we began barcoding our documents. I became the guru of the department and took on the role of mastering the new technology. The number of hours that I could work as a temporary employee, ran out for the year. As a temporary, I only was allowed to work so many hours in a year, or they had to hire me full-time. They hired me through an outside temporary agency to keep me on the project.

Our department began growing rapidly from a two-person department to a four-person department. They hired a temporary girl full-time before they hired me. I thought it was unfair, a most likely discrimination, but I needed a job and remembered why I was there in the first place. *I was proving myself for my next job…*

Then, they began hiring internal company employees. Now, we had six to eight employees. We went from one shift to three shifts. Finally, I was hired full-time a year and a half later. Yippee! Hooray! I proved my friends and family wrong. I could be hired in a white, male-dominated company. If you have a dream or a desire to do something, keep persisting and follow through for it is waiting for you.

With all the new employees, I noticed a theme of happiness from the people at my work. I am a people watcher. As a child, my mother did not have a lot of money, so we would go to the mall and watch people. In watching my co-workers, I realized I wanted some of that happiness myself.

We had Christians, a Mormon, and a Jehovah's Witness in our little work group. The Jehovah's Witnesses woman had a great smile and was full of Joy. We would go to sit on the grass and talk about God. She invited me to attend one of her meetings. I dragged my mother with me, and we were the only two Hispanics. The meeting was in her basement, and they did not talk to us. We just sat there talking between ourselves. Kind of strange.

The Mormon woman was so funny. She was full of joy from deep within. One time, she came in early and went straight to the closet room. She said, "Do NOT look at me! I do not have my eyebrows on." She had not painted them on yet. (I must admit; she did look odd with no eyebrows.) She was married and was always spying on her husband because he was cheating.

How sad to live a life being cheated on. I know this scene all too well.

My father cheated on my mother. Then, my stepfather, Ben, kept sneaking around with his ex-wife for 20 years. I could never understand why my mother put up with that all those years.

The Christian women were so happy and full of something that I knew I wanted. They had a peace within them that radiated love. I was lucky to have three of them in my department. They talked about God, and how He was their friend, their comforter, and their light. I was like a sponge and soaked in every word. These three women would significantly change the direction of my life.

One of the Christian women, Debbie, became a great friend. She invited us to church for a revival one night. My mother and I were baptized that evening. We gave our life to Christ, and it was wonderful. It was a process that took many years to get the full understanding about the love of God. He loves us so deeply, it is amazing.

I have done so many bad things, and I was not worthy of his love. Yet, they taught me the love of God. He loved me and forgave all my sins. When I began to understand that there was nothing I could do to prevent God's love for me, that it is always there, the door opened up in my soul, and I changed.

I wanted to serve Him and live a life for Him. I am not perfect. However, I know that I am loved and that changes everything.

TRUST THE

Janiece's Life Lessons

➢ Life may not be fair, but be patient for your day will come.

➢ Be a people watcher. Find the people who are truly genuine and happy. Learn what gives them their inner happiness; then let them nourish your spirit.

➢ God loves you no matter what you have done. Let Him in, and He will change you.

CHAPTER 9

The Tease "Lead Position"

> "Step out of yourself made boundary and step into your new frontier."
> ~ Janiece Rendon

I took the graveyard shift doing data entry. I would have liked to have stayed on days; however; I was low man on the seniority list. They hired a temporary person to work with me. At the same time, they gave me a job title of "Lead Person" or something like that. I was told I was being promoted, but that they could not give me a pay raise. I did not care, I had a title. I was the Lead in a department. I felt like I was somebody. I was the connection between all three shifts. I made sure all shifts worked together to complete the process of filming and barcoding the documents. They sent me to Chicago for a week to master the new barcoding system. I felt like I was someone important and that was what mattered.

The big boss was another mentor in my new journey. His name was Don, and he was so smart. He could literally calculate numbers in his head without a calculator. I was so impressed. When I became a full-time employee, I bought a house. He said, "Janiece that is great. Now we own you," and he smiled. He had an open door, and he loved to talk. I would take it all in making mental notes.

He said, "Janiece, one day people will be planting gardens in their yards, so you need to have land to farm your own crops." He talked about many things, and I stored them in my memory for future knowledge. Then one day, Don called me in his office. He said, "Janiece we have to take away your title."

I admit, I was a little shocked, as the title had not come with a pay raise. I guess there were some people in mid-management that could not accept someone like me in charge.

I refused to let that upset me. After all, I was there to prove myself for my next job. I continued as the lead, meaning I was the contact person. I knew the system inside and out. One thing I learned from this situation was **knowledge is power**. Learn as much as you can, because no one can ever take away your knowledge. When they are coming to you for the solution or answers, it does not matter if you have the title or not, you are in charge.

It felt good to be the person in charge.

TRUST THE Curves

Janiece's Life Lessons

- Do not let a title become your importance; it can be taken away in an instant.

- If you have the opportunity to be around amazing people; take the time to learn as much as you can, for they are a gift.

- If you know your importance deep within, the naysayers may win and taking away your title; however, you still have the knowledge.

- Knowledge is power.

CHAPTER 10

The Power of Determination

> "You can be anything you want to be if you just help enough other people get what they want."
>
> ~ Zig Ziglar

Management had a new concept and wanted everyone to experience different shifts, so, we began taking turns rotating shifts. Little did I know, this was going to be the moment that would change my life forever. Marilyn, one of the Christian women, came from the day crew to work with me on graveyard.

First, take a moment to picture this. There I was, sitting with my feet on the desk, laptop in my lap, a bandana on my head, chewing watermelon bubble gum, and listening to the oldies with my headphones.

After a couple of nights of watching this, Marilyn said, "Janiece, I have something for you to listen to."

I said, "Okay." I popped in what was an audio cassette of Zig Ziglar, a famous motivational speaker. As I listened to the cassette tape, I heard a man who talked fast and said, "You can be anything you want to be if you just help enough other people get what they want."

I thought to myself, "This is good for him, her, or other people, but Zig, you do not know who I am. And, Zig Baby (as I called him), you are going to tell me I can do anything I want to do if I just help enough other people get what they want?? Right." I'm seriously thinking this man is insane. However, there was something about him that I just couldn't put my finger on. There was something in his voice that made me believe him. So, I continued listening. One night, what he was saying sunk in. I decided right then and there that I, Janiece Rendon, was going to be the next Zig Ziglar.

I was so excited! I could picture myself standing in front of an audience changing lives.

The next morning, I went to the other office to meet the day crew. I was on fire, I am telling you! I had a smile from one side of my face to the other. One of the girls asked me, "Who do you think you are, with all that positive attitude stuff acting like you are somebody?"

I wanted to tell her, "Did you not you hear what Zig Baby told me last night? He told me I can be anything I want if I just help enough other people get what they want." But, I kept my mouth shut because I knew she would not understand. However, the dream was planted firmly in my soul. I was going to be the next Zig Ziglar and nothing was going to stop me. Nothing.

Now, the real work was to begin. I had a lot of work to do. I needed experiences to teach from. (Be careful what you ask for, because the life experiences you ask for will show up! And, little did I know what was coming my way.) I needed an education. I needed to join Toastmasters, a public speaking organization. Oh I was going to be busy! That night changed my direction in life. I was going to change the world.

I was on fire!

* * * * *

I kept up my new attitude. I was going to be happy no matter what. Titles can be taken away, people can make fun of me, it did not matter, I now had a purpose. I had bigger and better things ahead of me. I had things to finish like completing my high school diploma.

I walked across the stage after high school ended, but the diploma I received was blank.

I wanted to go to college, but in order to go to college I needed to have a diploma or G.E.D. I called my high school to find out how to get my diploma. Even though I had more credits than I needed to graduate high school, I was ½ credit short in Physical Education. I thought that should count for something, right? The person at the high school said, "Yes that is correct. You do have more credits than what is required. However, Physical Education is a required course and you need to complete that half credit to graduate."

I said, "Okay, great, I will go back to high school to take a P.E. class." She informed me that I was past the age of 21 and could no longer attend high school. She said that my only option was to get a G.E.D. That was not an option for me.

I said, "I want my high school diploma from this high school." I asked to speak to someone higher in authority to work this out. She gave me a name and number, and I called them. Again, I was turned down with no hope. I was devastated. How was I going to go to college? I deserved to have my diploma. The wheels were turning. I thought, "How do I make that happen?"

I went to work the next day and told my boss the situation. I told him I wanted to go to college, but I did not have my diploma. What could I do? I am only a half credit short in Physical Education. He said, "You go to the Wellness Center correct?" (The Wellness Center is a gym for the company.)

I said, "Yes."

He said, "The Wellness Center monitors you with your badge when you enter. Write a proposal to your school to use your workouts for a half credit of Physical Education. Have the staff at the Wellness Center sign off on the hours."

I did not know how to write a proposal, but I could learn. I asked if he had a proposal I could look at. He gave me a company one and my writing began. I wrote the proposal, then went back to my high school and spoke with the same person. She said that a proposal for a half credit in P.E. was not possible. I asked to speak with someone else higher in authority. They agreed to accept this proposal, and I received my high school diploma in 1994.

> "When you have a mission, nothing is going to stop you."
> ~Janiece Rendon

The power of a determination is an amazing gift to open doors. It is funny, because people get confused when I fill out an application and write 1994 as my high school graduation date when it should have been 1978. They are not sure how old I really am! It's the world's best youth serum.

I was so excited to begin my new journey in college. Not only that, I was accepted at a major university.

I thought back to the woman who threw my application in my face telling me that I could not read or write. I thought to myself I must be able to write something, because I was accepted to a major university with my writing skills. Even though, I still hear her voice running through my ears every time I have to write a paper, or even write this book! Look at me!

Regis University had a special program for our corporate company. The instructors came onsite to teach our classes to obtain a certificate in Business Leadership. It was convenient, and I was able to make some great connections from other departments within the company.

The first class was fun; it was on finding your career passion. However, the next class was difficult.

The first day of class, the instructor told us he was very strict with grammar, spelling, and proper English. We had better know the difference between to, too and two. Again, I began to question my abilities in writing.

On our first break we went to the lunchroom. I had tears in my eyes and told a couple of friends, "I can't do this. I am not good at writing." They encouraged me to continue. They said, "You can do this!"

Again, I could hear that woman's voice drowning in my ears. It is sad how we let someone destroy our belief in ourselves through the power of words. The worst part about it is, we believe a stranger's words, and it haunts us for a lifetime. If I had known I would have had that same strict instructor for the next four or five classes, I probably never would have gone back to class after that first day.

It is extremely important to have supportive people around you to help you continue your journey. Find people who believe in you and will give you words of encouragement along the way. This is necessary in life. Build a team of people who will lift you up. Along your journey in life, there will be more people on the sidelines trying to destroy you then trying to help you. When you have a team of encouragers walking with you, the naysayers begin to fall away.

Janiece's Life Lessons

- ➢ Be brave enough to approach someone and give them hope. Who knows, you might just change their destiny.

- ➢ Your past is not your future.

- ➢ Form a picture in your mind of you standing in success. Before you know it, it will be reality.

- ➢ Do not be afraid to let your light shine!

- ➢ Get ready for an amazing life!

- ➢ Keep an attitude of gratitude.

- ➢ No does not always mean no.

- ➢ Ask someone you trust for an answer to your dilemma.

- ➢ The power of your determination will open doors.

- ➢ You can make things happen. Trust in yourself and follow through.

- Do not let someone else's words detain you from fulfilling your destiny.

- Build a team of encouragers to walk with you.

- You may question your abilities; however, do not stay there.

CHAPTER 11

Rock Bottom

> "Your thoughts are your most powerful asset."
> ~ Janiece Rendon

The Microfilm department was under scrutiny to get outsourced. We had an outside company come in and look at every detail of our processes. After months of due diligence, we were in the clear to continue microfilming in-house. As you see, we were a small department of eight people, we filmed insurance documents, payroll, purchase orders, and accounts payable for the whole company. We were very efficient at what we did. And despite that, every year we were threatened with outsourcing.

One time, we, along with the mailroom, and Forms Management, were so close to being outsourced. We were all gathered into the mailroom as one of the top managers let us know we were being outsourced. It was not a matter of "if" but "when." She stood up there with fake tears in her eyes and acted as if she was about to cry. I thought to myself, "Are you kidding me? Hold the theatrics for your personal life."

They brought in outside individuals to help each of us with resumes and career counseling. Although, we survived yet another year, we had to document every detail of our jobs. Yippee!

The woman with the fake tears was long gone and off to her next job with another company. We were still there.

* * * * *

They promoted me from Microfilm to Forms Management. I was in charge of all the forms for this giant company. As you can imagine, the company had many, many forms. In looking at some of the forms from different departments, we noticed that many of the forms were the same, but with different wording. As a department, we decided to consolidate all company forms to standardized forms. This process gave us the ability to eliminate the storage of forms from our offsite location. We began printing black and white forms on-demand when needed, instead of storing on shelves.

I worked with an outside company to begin eliminating our inventory. As we began using our vendor less, we began taking on the role of editing the forms. I was way in over my head with this role. I am not a detailed oriented individual. I began making mistakes. And, I knew it.

I did not have the experience to know what questions to ask and what to look for in the forms. I could feel the passion in my everyday work begin to dwindle. In the past, I had great reviews from management, and they praised me for the great work I did. Now, I did not feel good about what I was doing. I was drowning in despair.

Along with the despair, our management changed. I now had a new supervisor. When she came into the department, things began to change. My reviews went from being highly praised to being written up for everything I did wrong. She rarely acknowledged me. She got a new boss from outside the company. One day she was giving him a tour of our area and was introducing him to people.

She completely overlooked me and instead introduced him to a temporary from our department, then she moved on to the next room. What does that say to a new boss when you overlook an employee from the introductions? What does that say about me? It told me I wasn't important. I was already feeling unappreciated and my self-esteem began deteriorating. I felt like I was drowning and had no one to turn to for advice. My old mentors were gone.

She began writing me up on everything she could think of to do. The more she wrote me up, the more mistakes I made. It was a no win situation for me. I began feeling physically sick every time I had to go to work. I knew something was wrong, but wasn't sure what was happening.

I had a friend from another department ask me what was going on. She noticed my outlook on life had changed drastically. I was sad and depressed. She said I should go see my doctor. I had written a paper on depression for school, but now that I was experiencing it, it was much different than what I wrote about. I went to the doctor and they diagnosed me with depression.

I went to our in-house counselors, and they put me on a leave of absence for depression. They asked me how long I needed to be off work. I told them I did not know, but when I knew I was ready to come back, I would let them know. I had let everything get to me, and I was at my rock bottom. I went from an employee who was the guru of the department, to an employee who made mistakes and was treated poorly.

I had to see a therapist and go to group counseling every week. I was off work for five months. Every week, I went to group counseling, then a single session with my therapist. This situation was very difficult. I rather existed for five months avoiding life. I was ashamed and did not want to be around anyone. I felt like I had lost my edge. I felt like I was useless and worthless. Then, one session with my therapist changed my outlook.

The counselor said, "Janiece, sometimes when you're depressed that is just who you are."

I remember looking at her and thinking to myself, "WHAT?"

I was at a turning point in my life. I had a choice. Was I going to be a person who walked around life just existing? Or, was I going to be the next Zig Ziglar? It was a quick second moment in time, and the door was about to close. I needed to decide right NOW!

Who is Janiece?

I do not remember the rest of the session, but I knew I had a choice to make. I had already made that decision, a long time ago, "that one night working graveyard." I just had to reach inside to find the strength. I knew once the door closed it was over.

Who is Janiece?

This was going to be my defining moment. I closed the door on defeat! I knew what Zig Baby told me that one night working graveyard. He said, "I could be anything I wanted if I just helped enough people get what they want."

Well, I wanted to be the next Zig Ziglar, and I knew that this state of depression was not going to get me there. I had a mission and this circumstance was not going to define me. When I leave this company for good, I am going to leave on top. I will be darned if I am going to let someone take away everything I worked so hard to achieve. I am not done in this company. I am not done with my mission!

That was the last time I saw the therapist. I had taken control of my life again, and I was on fire!

TRUST THE

Janiece's Life Lessons

- ➤ When taking a promotion, be sure you have the job skills to do the job. If you are struggling, ask for help.

- ➤ If you are overlooked, have the courage to put out your hand, smile, and introduce yourself.

- ➤ Do not get comfortable in your position for it can change in a moment.

- ➤ Build your skill set for your next job.

- ➤ Even though you may be at your rock bottom there is only one way to go; and that is up. Do not give up.

- ➤ Remember you are Worthy!

- ➤ Close the door on defeat.

- ➤ Choose to leave on the top. Take control and let the fire relight your passion.

CHAPTER 12

Facing the Giant

> "You have inside you an amazing power that will help you leave the past behind and guide your tomorrow for an amazing adventure. Never under estimate your internal power, your internal power of God.
> **~Janiece Rendon**

I took my life back at that moment. I went back to work and told them I was ready to go to work. They asked how did I know I was ready? I said, "Remember when I was first going out on a medical leave and you asked when would I be ready to come back? I told you I did not know, but when I did, I would let you know. Well, I know I am ready, and I want to come back to work."

It was a big ordeal to get back to work. I had to meet with HR and find out how to return to work. They asked me if I wanted to go back to my same job in Forms Management (back to Microfilm), or I could go to a new department working in the Engineering Department as a file clerk.

I knew I did not want to go back to Forms Management. That job was not a fit for me. They meant well with a promotion. I felt that if I went back to Microfilm, it would be like I was going backwards; almost like a demotion. I thought about it and said, "I would like to go to the Engineering Department and be a file clerk." I was able to keep the same pay, so it would be a lateral move.

Then I was asked, "Do you want the same boss or a different boss?"

I said, "I want the same boss, no question about it."

"What??" you might be thinking. Most people would think I was crazy, because she was trying to get rid of me. However, I knew I had to face my demons and overcome them, or I would carry this defeat with me going forward.

Going back to face the same boss was one of the hardest things I have ever done. I remember my mom asking me, "How are you going to do it? How are you going to go back to work for the same lady that tried to fire you?"

I told her, "Mom, I don't know, but I do know that if I don't face this, I will take this defeat with me the rest of my life."

I knew I was an amazing person and that I was a great employee. I was in the wrong position, set up to fail, not intentionally, of course. Sometimes in life, we move in the wrong direction either by choice or by people making choices for us. I thought to myself, how much money and time could the company and I have saved if I could have been honest in the workforce and say, "I am struggling in this position," without the consequence of possibly losing my job.

Sometimes, people are promoted to move into management for the sake of promotion when they do not have the interpersonal skills to work with diverse group of people. Nor do they have the training to equip them. There should be diversity training for the managers who manage the people.

The best managers I worked with had the ability to guide the employee to thrive in areas they are good at. When this happens, there is a synergy and everyone wins.

Because I was able to take a look at my responsibility for the situation, I realized that was not the right position for me. When I came back to work, they had my personal stuff in a box. Someone had already moved into my position with her belongings in my space. In fact, it was a friend who had taken my job. It was a tough for me to see. However, I was back, and I was strong with inner strength.

Did my manager treat me fairly? Did management have an employee fit for the job? Both answers are, "No." Did we all learn from this experience? Yes! It was a win-win for both of us. As a matter of fact, we became friends. By looking at my part in the situation, I was able to give myself the power to overcome. Had I looked at the situation from a victim mentality, I would not have grown from the situation.

I believe both of us won in this situation. The power of forgiveness is so important in life. It can free you to move forward and be the person you were meant to be. Whether or not it was personal, did not matter. What mattered was how I took responsibility for my part in the situation, and how I forgave to overcome.

Because of the ability to look inside, I was able to get a chance to redeem my reputation of being a great employee once again. I went back to work part-time. They started me out working half days, then worked me back into full-time. I thought to myself, "I am going to be the best little file clerk I can be to prove myself for my next job." Actually, it was perfect; I filed papers and did not have to think. I put on my headphones, and of course, listened to my man, Zig Baby. He pumped me back up to the person I was supposed to be. I became that girl on fire again. I became the master of filing and learned as much as I could for my next job…

Janiece's Life Lessons

- Know who you are inside; then no one can stop you.

- When they are giving you choices; realize you have the power.

- Do not run from your problems. Face them eye-to-eye with courage and take back your power.

- Look at your part in a situation. It takes two to play the game.

- Swallow your pride and express your shortcomings. Sometimes we are in the wrong place and the situation is moving us toward our destiny.

- Do not get even; show them your strengths.

- The power to forgive is the key to your future.

CHAPTER 13

The Power to Ask for More

> You are on the right path, keep going forward what you need will find you."
> ~Janiece Rendon

I asked my boss after I was back on track, if I was doing a good job. One thing I realized is do not ask for something bigger until you master the job you currently have. I had to master the files before I could ask for more. I asked my boss if I could go work in Information Technology. I said I would do it on my personal time after work or during lunch.

You see, the key is to make sure you are doing a good job in the job you have, before you ask for more work or ask to move in a different direction. She gave her blessing and my journey was back on track. I began working for a wonderful person named Pat. She took me under her wing and used my skills as a file clerk. She felt bad for just having me file stuff at the beginning, but I said that was fine. She mentored me back to the direction of feeling worthy again.

A job opened up in Information Technology (I.T.) as a system administrator, and I applied. My boss recommended me for this position, and I was able to leave Engineering and move to I.T. I met two more amazing mentors, Mary and Debby. They gave me my wings and let me fly. Debby trusted me and let me do my job. Mary helped me with my reviews so that I was set up to win. I took over the cellphones for the company as well as helped with security backups and calling cards.

I.T. was in the process of being outsourced, as was the case in most companies. Of course, here we go again with due diligence and finding outside vendors who could take over our jobs to save the company money. I had this knack about landing under departments in the company that seemed to get outsourced. (I could not say that out loud or I might not get hired anywhere new.) We had a new CEO start with the company. He took all of the Information Technology team offsite to celebrate how much he appreciated us and thanked us for doing such a great job.

Then, it seemed like the next day we were in the process of being outsourced. We were told to meet in the conference rooms. There were different conference rooms, one for each quartile of the process. Depending on what room you were assigned to depended on if you were going to be laid off immediately, not yet, or not at all. I was in the room where we were going to be laid off, but not yet.

It was official, the Information Technology department was going to be outsourced. Four of us fell under the "outsourced, but not yet" category. We were going to reside under Finance until they could figure out what to do with our jobs.

We managed cell phones, company credit cards, and backing up files for the company. Going from I.T. to Finance was very interesting. The I.T. people were fun, and we were like a family. Finance people were different. They were very serious and did not talk very much.

At the time, cell phones were new and everyone wanted one. The company paid for company cellphones, and I noticed there were many non-business calls being made with company cell phones. I began questioning why we managed cellphones the way we did. It made more sense for the managers to monitor their employee's charges and cellphone calls in order to verify whether the charges were company related or personal. Before I knew it, I had outsourced a big portion of my position being efficient! Here I go again! I had two weeks before my vacation ran out to find another job. This time I was out, gone off the property, being paid for vacation while I looked for another job.

Janiece's Life Lessons

➢ God is in charge of your future. Times may get stressful however; He will take care of you.

➢ It is okay to speak up and find better ways to do something. You become more valuable to someone; even if it looks like you are working yourself out of a job.

➢ Do not ask to move somewhere else until your boss knows you can manage what you have.

➢ When you build trust in your management, they will recommend you to move on to better things.

➢ It never hurts to ask for more. The worst that could happen is they could say no. You will still be in the same place, so you did not lose anything.

CHAPTER 14

Attitude is Everything

> "Attitude is the key to your future."
> ~ **Janiece Rendon**

A friend of mine said, "Janiece, there is a job in Water Resources and Real Estate. Go take your resume to them today." I followed her advice and took my resume to the hiring manager. He was not there, so I left it on his desk. This was another example where I began to see my life connect itself in so many ways.

My stepfather wanted me to go to real estate school, so I followed his advice and attended Jones Real Estate school right after high school. I took my boards and missed by one or two questions. I could have gone back and taken the board exam again; however, it really was not my dream. So, it slipped by and life went on. Who knew going to real estate school was going to help me get a job many years later?

I went to the interview and there were about four people interviewing me and asking me many questions. The question that stood out the most was,

"Why do you have such a great attitude when you have been laid off from this company after working so many years?"

My response was, "I cannot control the circumstances of getting let go, but I can control how I react to the situation and keep my spirits high." Later, I was to learn from a co-worker that my attitude was what set me above all the other candidates.

In August 2002, I had been home for a few days looking for jobs outside the company. The distributing company I applied for hired me. A friend of mine had taken the job a couple of days prior then decided she did not want it because the pay was very low and you only got a one-week vacation. I was not thrilled about the pay either, but I needed to stay working in the area because my kids went to school nearby. I asked if I could buy a week's vacation. (We were able to do this in my prior job.) They said no, that was not in the benefits. I took the job and they ordered my airplane tickets to fly out to California for training on the following Monday.

I was on my way to pick up the tickets on Friday afternoon when my cellphone rang. It was my previous company calling to tell me that the Water Resources and Real Estate position was mine. He told me they would like me to start in two weeks. I was so excited to stay with the same company and keep my five week's vacation. He asked me what salary I was looking for, and I gave him a dollar amount. I pulled over to the side of the road. I had just accepted a job from my old company, and I was on my way to pick up airplane tickets for my new job. I was confused and did not know what to do.

I called my dad and said, "Dad, what do I do? I feel bad about not taking the job with the new company, but I have the opportunity to stay with the same company, keep my vacation time, and make more money."

He said Janiece, "Every company has a backup person they have in mind in case the first one does not work out. You have to do what is best for you."

I went in and told my new boss I accepted a job from my prior company. I told him I was sorry for such late notice, but I just accepted the job. He was upset, but understood.

I only had three days of vacation left. My old boss hired me back to do some filing and odd jobs, so that I would not lose seniority with the company.

Lesson learned: Never burn bridges.

Had I left the company with an attitude, I would not have been hired back by my old department to bridge the time until my new job began.

The first week with my new job, my boss asked me to set up a tour for our department to go tour the new distributing company. I about fell off my chair as the company he wanted to tour was the same place I had just turned down. I was hesitant to go at first, but decided to go with my new coworkers. Of course, as luck would have it, the person who was going to be my boss was our tour guide.

I told him, "This is the boss who stole me away from you." We all laughed. What were the odds?

Janiece's Life Lessons

➢ When someone tells you to apply for a job; jump and do it.

➢ Your past experiences can affect your future opportunities. Be sure to keep a list of experiences.

➢ Your attitude will take you farther than your experience or education.

➢ Every company has a backup plan. It is okay to change your mind and go for a better opportunity.

➢ Attitude is the key to all journeys in life.

➢ Humor will lead you out of some awkward situations.

CHAPTER 15

The Power of Tenacity

> "Life has many curved roads. You will eventually end up on the smooth road of life if you drive long enough. And, don't give up."
> ~Janiece Rendon

I had many challenges with this new job. I was in way over my head. I remember many times going to the bathroom and crying, asking myself, "What did I get myself into? I do not know what I am doing. I do not know how to do income statements and balance sheets."

The woman who trained me before she left, told me to just copy from the prior month and said, "You will be fine." She assumed I knew how to do financial statements. Well, I was not fine. I copied all right, however, I did not know what I was copying and made some huge errors. It was period-end, year-end. I remember handing over the balance sheet to my boss.

He looked at it and said, "Hmmm. I have never seen a negative balance in this area before."

I said, "Oh. Let me have it back. I might have made a mistake." A mistake well, yeah! I did not know what I was doing. I went back to my desk and began a detailed line item search from August, when the person who had worked before me, had made her journal entries. I found out where I made the first mistake and began correcting mistakes one-by-one. That was the night I stayed at work the entire night. Yes, 24 hours at work.

As I was working, the Excel spreadsheet I was using blew up. All the formulas disappeared, and I went into a panic. No matter what I tried, I could not recover the spreadsheet. I had to redo the entire Excel spreadsheet from scratch. I did not know Excel very well, and we are talking four months of financials. I was so tired and wanted to just lay down on the couch that was in the bathroom. But, I couldn't. I knew I had to fix the books. If I did not do it, who was going to do it? My boss probably did not know how to do them, so I had to figure it out.

When my boss walked in the next morning, which was a Friday, I was in the same clothes and tired. I told him I had been at work the entire night and figured out the problem, and I was going home. I had put in more than 24 hours in one day and was exhausted. I went home and slept. I went back to work on Monday and called some of my connections from Finance, who could help me get the books straight.

The woman who came in to look at the financials said, "You do not have the job skills to do this job."

I said, "I know. That is why I called for help."

She said, "I am going to have to tell your boss you do not have the job skills to do this job."

I told her that was not a problem, I was going to tell him as well. She was definitely a finance person, she had no sense of humor and kept on working. Every time she would find a mistake, she would shake her head. I just sat there like a puppy looking for some kind of approval; however, there was none from her. Oh, it was awful. I felt like an idiot, a loser and just downright stupid.

It took her a couple of days to get the books straight. If you have ever felt like the dumbest person in the world, you can relate. I felt like that the entire time she was there. On her last day, she said that she would be giving my boss a call to let him know that I do not have the job skills to continue with this position. I thanked her for getting the books back on track and we left it at that.

I was back from the holiday break. I was devastated and literally feeling at one of my lowest points in life. I think the worst part about it was that my boss saw something in me, but I felt like I was not stepping up to his expectations. I had only been in this position for four months and already had destroyed the books.

I could feel the tears at the back of my eyes ready to pour out when my boss walked in. He was a tall, gentle man, who had the calmest emotions. His emotions were steady at all times. I, on the other hand, had emotions that would go from high to low in an instant.

He walked by my desk and said, "Good morning, Janiece."

I muscled up the courage and told him, "Boss, you have to hire a new person. I do not have the job skills to do this job."

He continued to walk to his office without a word.

I sat at my desk trying to figure out if he was going to fire me. Should I start looking for a new job? Where would I go? What would I do? I continued working, trying to get my head wrapped around my daily tasks.

Finally, at 3:00 in the afternoon, my boss came out of his office and said, "Janiece, I did not hire you to be a CPA."

I thought to myself, "Are you kidding me? You wait until closing time to tell me this?" What I actually said to him out loud was, "Oh, thank goodness!" And, I smiled.

I had built a long list of connections within the company just like Faith had taught me to do, so I was able to ask for help. My boss suggested that I go to school to get an accounting degree. I told him accounting was not my strong point; however, I would go to school to get a business degree.

I enrolled in Accounting 101. We were talking about debits and credits, and the accounting part of my job began making sense. I told my teacher thank you for explaining accounting in layman's terms. Things began to connect and make sense. I felt more empowered to continue in my job with confidence. My boss was amazing and very patient with me while I learned the skills to do the financial portion of my job. The accounting part of my job was always a struggle.

Janiece's Life Lessons

- ➢ When you mess up, start from the beginning and retrace your steps to correct the problems.

- ➢ Do what you need to do to complete the project; no matter what it takes.

- ➢ Have many connections; you never know when you might need them.

- ➢ It is okay not to know how to do something. Find someone to help you; then educate yourself to figure it out.

CHAPTER 16

My Soul Mate Finds Me

> "Your life is your masterpiece choose the puzzle pieces carefully."
> ~Janiece Rendon

In 2006, my mother called me at work in a panic. She said, "Janiece, can you call a plumber?" There was a pipe leaking in the basement, and she could not fix it. That was a weird call because my mother could fix anything. I had watched her fix a washing machine.

I told her not to worry, that I would call the plumber right away. I called the plumber I usually use, but they were busy and could not come out that day. I looked in the phone book and called another plumber. I called my mom back and told her the plumber was on the way. She sounded relieved.

The plumber fixed the pipe, and she had him look at a few other things. While he was working, she made him a lamp out of one of our keg balls. On one of the projects he was working on for her, he told her that he did not have the parts and would have to call someone else to come fix it. He sat there while she finished the lamp.

She said, "Joe, I have a daughter who is single." She then proceeded to show him pictures of me and gave him my life history. He told her that he was going to go back to the office to pick up the parts, and he would be back to fix the faucet for her.

She called me and told me what she had done. I said, "You did what??" She laughed.

He came back and fixed her sink. He knew if someone else came out, that person might take advantage of her. In addition, I think he was hoping I would be home so he could check me out. However, I had to work late that night, so we missed each other. He called me the next morning at work and asked me how the pipes were doing. I laughed and said, "Now that is a line I have never heard before."

We talked for a few minutes, then he said, "Let's go to dinner tonight."

I said, "Well, we had this picnic at work today, and I have this huge table in the back of my truck." I hesitated, then I said, "Sure, why not?"

We met at Bennigan's in Arvada. I was so nervous as I drove to the restaurant. I wanted to back out. I pulled up in the parking lot and there he was, waiting in his truck. Well, I could not run now because I had this huge table in the back of my truck. It was obvious who I was.

We walked into the restaurant and sat down. We began talking, then ordered our drinks. He said that he had a seven-year-old daughter and if that was a problem, then we should end it right now.

I thought, "Wow!"

I told him that if we were laying it all on the table then he should know that I could not cook. So if he had a problem with that, then we should end it right now.

He asked me how I had found the number for his company. I told him that I had found it in the phonebook. He said, "That was impossible, they had made a mistake and the number was not printed in the yellow pages that year."

I said, "Well, that's odd. I was at work and looked it up in the yellow pages." We had a great dinner and talked for hours. We really connected. He had just come back to Colorado from San Diego in February. He said that he was not looking for a girlfriend. However, my mom was so nice that he thought, if I was anything like my mom, then I would be alright.

The next day I went to the file cabinet and looked at the yellow pages where I had found the plumber's number. It was a 1999 phonebook. Wow, were we meant to meet or what?

We have been together every day since, going on 10 years in 2016.

* * * * *

TRUST THE *Curves*

Janiece's Life Lessons

- It is okay to speak up for yourself in the beginning of a relationship.

- Take a chance on love. You never know where it might lead.

CHAPTER 17

Like the Whole World

> "Release people to change at their own pace and the change will take place in peace."
> ~Janiece Rendon

My mother began acting strange.

She was falling and could not start the car. (I found out later that she was asking the neighbor to start her car.) I took the keys away and told her if she could not start the car, she was not going to drive. Taking away her keys was one of the hardest things I had to do. She did not fight me too much, as she knew like I did that it was not safe for her to be driving.

My mom had just had surgery for a hernia a few months prior. When she came out of surgery, she was different. The doctors said that sometimes when elderly people have surgery the anesthesia takes a while to get out of their system. However, it was more than that, her speech began to slur. People thought my mom was drinking, but my mom did not drink.

Christmas morning, I made pancakes. We ate at the table, but my mom wanted to stay on the couch and watch TV. We were talking when all of a sudden my mother began choking. She could not breathe and was starting to turn blue.

I freaked out!

I was on the phone with 911, and Joe was trying to revive her. She passed out and fell in his arms. The life was gone from her body, and she was blue. Joe stuck his fingers down her throat and revived her. He said that he could feel the life come back into her.

She came to, looked up at him, and said with such thankful and loving eyes, "You saved my life."

Oh my gosh, it was a precious moment. I told 911 she was okay, and we hung up. I am not good in a crisis, especially when it is someone close to me.

* * * * *

January 2007, my mother was still acting strange. I had taken her to doctor after doctor trying to figure out what was wrong with her. I made an appointment at University Hospital with Geriatrics. The doctor went through the normal process. He tapped her knee with that silver thing and her knee jumped *very high*. I thought that was odd, I had never seen that before. He excused himself and said that he would be right back. In what seemed like a long time, he returned with a group of doctors. They examined her again, and the same thing happened. The doctors left, and we sat in the exam room.

The doctor returned. He said, "I think your mother has A.L.S. (Amyotrophic Lateral Sclerosis), or Lou Gehrig's disease, and it is fatal. Eventually, she will not be able to walk or talk, and she will become a vegetable. Her muscles will die and she will not be able to swallow."

I began to cry. He said, "I do not know for sure, but that it is what I think. Do not cry."

I said, "Doctor, I am crying because someone is actually paying attention to me. My mom has been acting strange for awhile now. They blamed it on old age, depression, and then anesthesia from the surgery. However, I knew it was something more."

I knew my mom, and she was different. I was in shock. My mother was going to die from this disease. We got in the car. Thoughts were running through my mind. I wanted to hear her say one more time that she loved me.

So I said, "Mom do you love me?" There was silence…

It seemed like a lifetime before she spoke and then she said, "Like the whole world." I will cherish those words until the day I die. "Like the whole world…" The most beautiful words to my ears.

I took her back to University Hospital to be tested and make sure that was what she had. They poked her and did all these tests on her. They were going to do this one test on her, and she wanted me to come in with her because she was scared. The nurse said no, that I had to wait in the waiting room, as the room was too small.

She came out and was crying. She said that it hurt so bad. They poked her with needles and kept asking her if she could feel it. It was as if she was the child, and I was the mother. The look in her eyes, full of pain and the unknown, was awful to see. I was an only child so I was it. I had this all on my shoulders. I was told hospice needed to come in.

Hospice brought in all this equipment: a bed, a walker, oxygen, and "the box." Hospice was there off and on, but not full time. I was told she had one year to live.

I began my calculations. I only had twelve weeks of vacation and Family Medical Leave time off. What was I going to do? Joe would stop in and look after her between his calls. Sometimes, he would have to pick her up off the floor and help her to the couch. It was so painful to watch her deteriorate in front of my eyes. I worked odd times. Some days, I only worked half days if she was having a bad day.

* * * * *

Life can be crazy and at the time my mother was dying, I had more strife in the family. I took custody of two of my aunt Debbie's girls again. Over the years, I helped raise five out of six of her children while she was in jail or prison. When I took custody of these two girls the first time, they were in first and third grade. I remember the day I brought them home. I was driving, my mom was on the passenger's side, and the girls were in the backseat. The oldest one was crying so hard and kept saying she wanted her mom. I knew it was hard for her.

The youngest one said, "What are you crying for?"

The oldest said, "I miss my mom."

The youngest said, "I miss my mom, too, but you do not see me crying."

Oh my gosh, it was so sad. The oldest one knew her mom. The youngest one had not bonded with her mother at all, as her mother was in prison soon after she was born.

They had grown up being with me on the weekends and all of the holidays. I did not think she would take it this hard. Many times, I would pile them in the back of the truck and off we would go to California, Texas, Montana, and even Mexico. However, the oldest daughter had a hard time actually making the permanent move to my home.

I remember one time at my grandmother's house, their mom was in the kitchen, and I said, "Mom," and asked my mom a question. The youngest was in my mom's arms and said, "Is this your mom?"

I said, "Yes."

She said, "Oh, no, this is my mom. Your mommy is in the kitchen." She wanted her mom to be my mom. I do not think she really understood what a mom was, but she claimed my mother as her mother. She loved my mom, and it was really going to be hard on her when my mom died.

One time, my aunt got in a motorcycle accident, and we took the girls to see their mother. The accident happened about a year before my mother was on her deathbed. I knew at that moment, I had lost my oldest daughter. Her heart was with her mother and she wanted to visit her mom every day. Her mother's leg was injured, but it was not a life-threatening situation. When my oldest was about to become 18, she began giving me many problems. We had a blow out one day after work and she said, "I'm leaving."

I told her, "You have to do what you have to do." She went to live with her mom. I was very sad, and it was so hard for my youngest daughter. She loved her sister, and now she was gone.

One time I was reading a text from my oldest daughter on my youngest daughter's phone. She said, "Does Dr. Phil (meaning me) know we are talking?" I cracked up and thought, "Wow! I'm famous."

* * * * *

Joe and I were out to dinner one night when the nurse called me. She said, "Janiece, your mom is not doing well, it is time."

I thought to myself, "Time for what?" When I left her in the morning, she was fine. I thought this nurse must be doing drugs (You know, they have access to many drugs. I thought she must be a druggie.) We left dinner and came home. My mom seemed okay when we got there.

Joe is such an amazing person. He brought up a mattress from the basement so I could hold my mother's hand all night. And his daughter, Adrianna, took off my mother's socks and rubbed lotion on her feet as she often did. (Now that, was an amazing young lady.) We went to sleep. That night, my mom was having a really hard time. I called hospice, and they said it was time. It was time for "the box."

"The box" was a mix of drugs to help the patient in their last days. I was to give her .75 milligrams of morphine or something like that. I did not know anything about drugs, so I ran downstairs and woke up Joe. Joe was a diabetic, and I knew he could do the right dose without killing her. We pulled out "the box" from the back of the fridge, and he filled the dose and gave it to her under her tongue. She was now calm and able to sleep. Joe began sleeping with me on the floor next to my mom.

I was no longer working. I had to care for my mother 24 hours a day now. My mother knew the power of relationships. People would come visit her at all hours of the day and night. She worked in the bakery for 30 years, and she was loved by so many. She touched many lives and they all wanted to give her their respect by honoring her last days.

Even my Aunt Debbie and the kids would come over and visit my mother. There were some harsh words spoken after my oldest daughter left to go visit her mother. We did not talk to each other. The tension in the house was so thick, I would literally go to the back room while they visited with my mom.

Joe used to get so mad and said, "This is your mother, you should not have to leave while they get to visit her."

However, I knew this was not about me. This was about my mother, and they needed to visit her in her last days as well.

* * * * *

I was exhausted. I was greeting people, taking care of my mother, cooking, and cleaning. Joe and the kids helped when they were home, but it was taking a toll on me. Not thinking clearly, I told Joe one day, "You and Adrianna have to leave! Do you not see your daughter is going to experience death? My mom is dying. This is not fair to Adrianna. Getting close to my mom, and then she will die. She should not have to witness death."

Joe said, "No my dear, she is witnessing love. You are showing my daughter the gift of love by taking care of your mother and loving your mom through this process."

He was so smart and observant, that is why I love him.

One day, I asked my cousin if she would watch my mother while I took a quick shower. I told her I would not dry my hair, I just needed a shower. I had been so busy, I was not able to even take a shower. She said she would be honored to help. We began going through old DVDs looking for one of my cousin's wedding pictures. We loaded a DVD and on it was my mom and Ben's wedding. The Mariachis started playing, and I am telling you, my mom opened up her eyes and enjoyed the music. She loved Mariachis.

That was the last time she was coherent.

Death is interesting. I could watch her fade in and out of this world and see her looking to the next life. I would curl her hair with her pink and green soft foam rollers. (My mother rolled her hair every night since she was a child. She did not like her straight hair.) We laughed because my rollers were placed crooked in her hair and not in order. My mother was so good at rolling her hair, she could do it in the dark without a mirror and have perfect rows. What a great memory…

Janiece's Life Lessons

➢ Learn to let go.

➢ Sometimes, the best thing to do is step aside; it is not always about you.

➢ Have the tenacity to continue searching for someone who will believe you in helping with your loved ones.

➢ Never be afraid to ask, "Do you love me?"

➢ Appreciate the small acts of love. Small memories could be the Best memories.

➢ Ask for help if you do not know how to do something.

➢ The power of having friends is a blessing; make sure to connect with people.

CHAPTER 18

The Gift of Forgiveness

> "Pluck out the poison of unforgiveness and let your heart blossom with love."
>
> ~ Janiece Rendon

One year on Christmas Eve, my step-dad, Ben, left my mother to return to his ex-wife. One of his daughters wanted her mom and dad together, so she kept pushing her dad to go back to her mother, and eventually, he did. He had been seeing his ex for the last 20 years anyway, and my mom knew about it.

Well, it was an awkward situation, and his kids did not talk to us after that. They treated my mom badly when we saw them on the street. It was like we had this huge family, and then we did not. It was a very awkward situation.

On my mother's deathbed, my stepsisters and stepbrother came to give her their last respects. My stepfather had already passed away. After all the years of pain my mother had endured, it was such a blessing to witness the greatest gesture of all, their presence and forgiveness in action. She was now released from the grief, and appreciated for the giving of herself through the years. They gave my mother the best gift they could. They gave her the gift of respect and acknowledgement of life. Her life had been complete, and all the people she loved and cared for had visited her.

I was showing one of them the house, when my mother took her last breath. I believe she waited until I left the room to die. I came upstairs, and there she was in the front room, gone.

On my mother's last days, there were birds on the tree across the street. They were so loud and chirped all day and night. When she took her last breath, there was silence. The birds were gone and never returned.

Kind of like the day my mom was lying on the bed in the front room, and she told Joe, "Bird." She could not talk very well. The disease had settled in the muscles of her throat.

He said, "Yes. Bird," and pointed at our fake bird.

She said, "No. Bird," and gestured with her eyes up behind the curtain. Joe moved the curtain and sure enough, there was a real bird in the house! He chased the bird out of the house.

You know the saying, "If there is a bird in the house, it means death."

Well, death came and the birds were gone from the tree, and the chirping stopped.

Janiece's Life Lessons

- When someone walks out of your life; let them go. If it was meant to be they will return; if not, go on with your life and enjoy the gift.

- Forgiveness is the true freedom to gift another individual.

- Paying respect in a person's last days is an ultimate gift of love.

CHAPTER 19

I Am Strong

> "No matter how much you prepare in life there will be surprises you did not plan. Remember you will manage through it."
> ~ **Janiece Rendon**

I always thought to myself when my mother died I would lose it. She was my best friend. I was so blessed to have her in my life. I remember one time when my mother and I got into a fight, we went for a walk the park. She was walking behind me when my aunt called me. My aunt asked me what we were doing, and I told her that we were fighting.

She said, "You guys fight?"

I am like, "Yeah. Everyone fights. However, when you respect the relationship, you make things work." About half way around the park, we were talking again.

I love you, Mom, rest in peace!

One of my friends thought I would fall into a deep depression. I had been preparing myself for her passing. I planned each step of death in my head. I knew what was going to happen, how it was going to happen. I mentally was prepared.

However, I did not plan two things that were very hard for me. The first was when they came to take away her body. They covered up her head, then loaded her in the vehicle and drove away. The covering of her head was the final stage of her being gone, and I had not planned this part in my head. It was so hard.

I started to run towards the car, and was saying, "Don't go." I suddenly caught myself as Joe took me back into the house. It was then that I wanted everyone to leave. This was my moment with my mom. I wanted her all to myself.

However, so many people loved her, and I knew I had to share her one last time. The neighbors were walking up the stairs to see how she was doing as they were carrying my mom out. The look on their faces was shock, then they looked at me to make sure I was okay.

I went to the funeral home before everyone came and there she was lying in the casket with bright red lipstick on. Now, I was in shock! My innocent mother was lying there looking like a hoochie. I began taking off her lipstick. My mother always wore maroon lipstick, not bright red. The woman from the funeral home saw what I was doing and told me if I used my lipstick, I would have to destroy it. Something about the embalming fluid. I didn't care. I did it anyway. We fixed her up and the service began.

The next day was the actual funeral and the final viewing of my mother. People were in line for what seemed like forever to say their goodbyes. Joe and I were the last to see her before they closed the casket. The second thing I was not prepared for, was for them to make the final closure of the casket. All I remember saying was, "Moooommmm."

A friend from work told me my voice echoed throughout the church, and it was heart wrenching. Joe took my shoulder and eased me to my seat. The rest of the services, I was prepared for, the cemetery and the lowering of the casket. We had Mariachis at her funeral. It was beautiful.

Janiece's Life Lessons

➢ You are stronger than you think.

➢ Everyone fights. There are no perfect relationships. The key is respecting the relationship to continue forward.

➢ In the midst of the seriousness of life, it is okay to see the humor. It breaks up the pain.

CHAPTER 20

The Proposal

> "Step out of your fear of commitment; life is short."
>
> ~ Janiece Rendon

Joe proposed to me on our first year anniversary, August 2nd, 2007. It was so romantic. I knew he was going to do it because his daughter kind of spilled the beans with excitement. We went to go eat at Black Angus Steakhouse. He got down on one knee. He gave me a Taco Bell sauce packet that said, "Will you marry me?"

I said, "Yes!" and the people clapped.

He thought it was corny, but I thought it was romantic. (I still have that taco sauce packet.) But the truth was, I wasn't ready to make that kind of commitment. It would take me another six years before I would say, "I do."

I had this thing with commitment. I had seen so many marriages break up. I saw how my father and stepfather treated my mother. I did not want to get hurt.

In addition, Joe had diabetes, and I was scared of the disease. I saw my stepfather give himself shots, and then he died of the disease anyway. I remember thinking that I did not want someone who was sick. I was afraid. Then I realized, who knows what life holds for any of us?

I asked myself, "What if I got in an accident and was brain damaged? Would he be the kind of man that would stick by me?" I knew in my heart he would. I saw how he helped me take care of my mother, and he only had known her a few months.

* * * * *

Joe went to the doctor for a regular diabetes appointment. They drew his blood. The woman came in the room and told him he was going into kidney failure and needed a kidney transplant, then proceeded to walk out of the room. As he sat there in shock, the doctor came in and Joe told him what the woman said. Joe said that she must have had the wrong room. The doctor said, "No, she was right. You need a kidney transplant."

They scheduled him immediately for surgery to get a fistula ready to begin dialysis. It all happened so fast, we were in shock. He told me, "You do not have to stick around. I have so much baggage: a young child, health problems, and now I need a transplant."

I told him, "Are you kidding me? You did not know my mother, and you were there for her and me. You would stop in and check on her between calls. I do not know what I would have done without you. I love you, and I am here for you."

I knew in my heart he would be there for me. I witnessed it with my mother.

The wait began.

Joe was officially on the list for a kidney/pancreas transplant. Because he was a Type 1 diabetic, he could go for both organs. The pancreas would give him a diabetic-free life. A kidney transplant had a waiting list of five years or longer. For both a pancreas and kidney transplant, the wait was much shorter; 6 months to a year. We could no longer travel very far while waiting for the call. We had to be ready at all times to be at the hospital within two hours after receiving the call.

We packed a bag and had it by the bed ready to go to the hospital. Life went on as usual, and we began to let it sit in the back of our minds. We were coming back from Montrose, Colorado after visiting Joe's dad, when on our way home, our Tahoe broke down in Glenwood Springs. We got a hotel room to spend the night until the automotive shop opened up in the morning.

Wouldn't you know it, Joe got the call. He was a backup recipient for a transplant. This meant that if the other person was not a perfect match, he would get the organs. He needed to get to the hospital to get prepped for surgery. We began freaking out; it was late in the afternoon when our vehicle had broken down. The car rental places were closed. We did not know anyone from Glenwood Springs. I was ready to hitchhike. However, we had our girls with us.

Joe called his dad from Montrose to come drive him to Denver for the transplant. His dad came to pick him up and before they went, I was kissing Joe not knowing if it would be the last time I saw him. The girls and I stayed in the hotel alone in Glenwood Springs that night hoping everything would be okay. It was a long night.

The other person was a perfect match so Joe did not get his transplant that evening. They came back to Glenwood Springs. We fixed the Tahoe, and we were back to our normal everyday lives. When we got back home, we made sure to check our hospital bag to make sure we had everything. With the backup transplant call, we knew that at any moment we could get a call, and our lives would change forever. All of a sudden, the reality of a transplant was in the front of our minds.

A couple of months later, Joe's dad asked if Adrianna could spend a few weeks with them in Montrose, Colorado. It was early June, and we drove her to Montrose to visit. We got home to unwind from the long drive and the phone rang. It was the middle of the night. Joe looked at the phone number, and it was University Hospital. He sat straight up and said, "Hello?"

The woman on the other end of the phone told Joe, "We have a match for a kidney/pancreas. As soon as we make sure that everything is a go, we will call you back. Now, get some sleep."

Get some sleep?? Are you kidding us? The excitement and the fear all began to sink in. We jumped out of bed and scrambled around like crazy people making sure we had everything in the bag.

Joe ran downstairs and told Cherrelle, my youngest daughter, "We got it! We got it! The kidney and pancreas! We will wake you up again as soon as they call us back." On the way down the stairs to tell Cherrelle, Joe heard a loud pop from his foot. He thought, "I am not going to say anything. I want this transplant."

He had pulled the tendon in his foot, but the adrenaline from the call kept him going. Joe limped up the stairs. We laid in bed praying and thanking God (along with the donors) for this amazing gift while we waited for the phone to ring. The phone finally rang, and she told us we needed to be at the hospital in an hour.

No problem, it was early morning, around 3:00 am, so there was no traffic. We headed off to University Hospital full of hope and joy. Joe gave himself a shot of insulin and said, "Just think, this is my last shot. How awesome is that?" and he smiled.

Janiece's Life Lessons

- Waiting is a part of life. Get used to living in the wait.

- You never know when you will see someone for the last time; tell them you love them often.

- Prayer and giving thanks in advance will give you peace when times are stressful.

- Life is short; live your life to the fullest.

- It is okay to be corny; you create a life memory.

CHAPTER 21

The Gift of Life from Our Donor "Thank You."

> "Don't take for granted the joy of waking up. Live!"
>
> ~ Janiece Rendon

We arrived at the hospital, they prepped him for surgery, and we waited, and waited, and waited. His surgery did not happen until late morning. In the hospital there were four families waiting for transplants. The person who had died was saving four people's lives that day. How awesome was that? The surgery was long and the waiting was tough. I kept thinking I could not lose him. God, I just lost my mom two years ago, what would I do if I lost Joe, too?

I had the most amazing family take care of me and was there for me while he was in surgery. The Lopez family would take turns to make sure someone was with me so I would not be alone.

As I was sitting there, I looked up, and around the corner I saw my mother. I had to look twice, for I knew it was not my mother. My cousin was wearing my mom's jacket. When she came around the corner, I thought it was my mom. I believe that was a sign my mom was there with me. She wanted me to know.

Surgery was finally over and the doctor came out and said the surgery was a success. Joe was in recovery. Oh, my goodness! What a relief to know he was alive and well. I went in to see him, and he was still groggy. He said, "See I told you I was going to be okay."

I said, "I know. I love you!" I told him I was going to run home and take a shower, but I would be right back. I took my shower and the phone rang. It was Joe, he was going back into surgery. The pancreas had a blood clot, and they were going to remove it. I freaked out and felt bad for leaving the hospital. I rushed back to the hospital, and he came out of surgery doing well. He said, "I am still a diabetic. They reconnected my old pancreas, and removed the new one."

The doctor said that the most important organ was the kidney, so we were happy. Joe was in the hospital for about four days before they released him to come home. I was now going to become the nurse. His incision was from his chest to his groin. They did not completely sew it back together because it had to heal from the inside out. I could literally stick my thumb in each hole, that was how much the wound was open.

It is amazing to witness how awesome our bodies are made. The body begins to heal itself by forming puss pockets like round balls. Then they form together to heal the wound, and it begins to close. The true gift of life was right in front of my eyes. I cannot thank the donor family enough for saving my husband's life.

We wrote them a letter, but we never heard anything from them. All we know was that it was a man who was in an accident and had died. Because this man was a donor and his family honored it, four people were able to live that day on June 15, 2009. What a blessing.

They gave me a pencil sheet with all the medication Joe would be on for the rest of his life. I carefully looked it over to make sure I knew how to make his daily pills. I was so scared. What if I got it wrong and killed him?

The morning and evening pills were different, so I had to pay attention. We went to the hospital every day for blood work to make sure the kidney was okay. Then every other day, then once a week, etc. I had been in charge of his pills for a while now. I knew them like a book.

Then one day, Joe was acting really mean and angry. Adrianna and I could not say anything without him getting upset and yelling at us. We were scared to breathe around him. Thank goodness, we were going to the hospital once a week. I told the nurse and doctor how he was acting, that his anger was out of control. I pulled out the pencil sheet, and sure enough it was my fault. I had made a huge mistake. I had given him steroids in his morning pills and again in the evening pills. I was giving him a double dosage of steroids. Yep, I was to blame for his mood swings.

Joe thought it would be a good idea if he began doing his pills, and I would be the backup pill maker. I was relieved. My daughter, and I were fine with that. We joke about this all the time now. Joe told me I was trying to kill him. I said, "No, I was trying to commit suicide, because my daughter and I were the ones who suffered."

It was a tough time. And, it was a great time. We got to witness firsthand the gift of life.

God has been with me my whole life. I have been in situations in my life that could have been fatal for me; however, God kept me alive to be there at that moment to nurture the love of my life back to health. Joe used to get mad at me because I would not let him do things. I told him he needed to recover and rest, but he was tired of resting and wanted to do something. He wanted to feel manly and do something with his hands.

I told him to rest, it was part of the process. He was so ready to be healthy and feel like a man, that he built a shed in the backyard with two rooms. The neighbor thought it was a rental house. I was so mad at him when I came home from work. However, I knew he needed to do that for inner healing.

Before the transplant, Joe had no energy. He would get up in the morning, take a shower, and feel exhausted. He could not work because he had no energy. We found a picture of him standing in front of the fireplace, and he literally looked like he was the walking dead. He was pale and grey. He was sick.

God will provide the strength to help you through anything you go through in life. I was able to witness God do miracles in our lives. I know God planned for us to meet. If this would have happened while he was alone, he would have kept working, and it would have killed him.

He was raising Adrianna alone, so in order for him to survive he would have worked to keep a roof over her head and food in her tummy. By us being together, Joe had the ability to trust in the Lord, stop working until he received his transplant, and heal. I honestly do not know how we made it financially. But, we did. I know God provides. I witnessed God in our lives through the whole process. God is good all the time!

Joe began getting his strength back. He had to change his profession from a plumber because he could no longer work with all the bacteria. Joe had always been a mechanic, so that was the natural path for him to follow. He went back to school to get his certification in mechanics, and was on the honor roll for every class. Joe knew so much about mechanics that the other students would come to him with questions.

Life is good and the one thing we need to take seriously is our health. I am in the process of getting my health in check. Check out my daily walks with Janiece on Facebook. It is one of my daily commitments to myself.

Janiece's Life Lessons

- ➤ Sign up to be a donor; you can give a miracle to many people.

- ➤ The power of prayer is the key.

- ➤ Give the gift of time; for it is the most treasured gift of all.

- ➤ Give your loved one's clothes to family. For one day, you never know when that jacket or piece of clothing will give you comfort and hope.

- ➤ The gift of life is amazing!

- ➤ Our bodies are an amazing gift from God.

- ➤ Be patient and love your loved ones while they heal back to health.

- ➤ Believe in miracles.

- ➤ There is a reason why lives cross paths; trust the process.

- ➤ Our health is precious.

CHAPTER 22

Thanksgiving Wedding

> "Step out of yourself made boundary, and step into your new frontier."
>
> ~ Janiece Rendon

I went to a conference that changed my life. I was talking to the "Drill Sergeant of Life" about my fear of commitment. I told her how Joe was getting upset and wondering if I ever was going to marry him.

She drew an imaginary line. I was on the side of fear, and she told me to step over it. She literally had me step out of fear. It affected me so much, I went home and asked our daughter if I could ask her dad to marry me. She said, "Sure, but the boy should ask girl, right?"

I said, "Yes, and he did six years ago." She gave her blessing and was happy. I went into the dining room where Joe was sitting and said, "Let me have your ring."

He looked at me strange, said, "Okay," and took it off.

I got down on my knees and asked him to marry me. I said, "Let's get married on Thanksgiving, because I am so thankful for you in my life." We decided to get married in Las Vegas, and got married on November 26, 2013. We spent a week in Las Vegas, just the three of us. Adrianna was our witness. After the ceremony, we left her in the hotel, and the two of us spent the day together.

When we came back to the hotel there was wine, chocolate covered strawberries, roses, and more roses. Our friends, and my dad and stepmom sent these amazing gifts of love to our hotel because they were not able to be with us. It was so very special.

My daughter was so cute. She said, "You should tell dad you are pregnant." We were texting back and forth as we were walking the strip. She was telling me to do this the day after we got married. She was so serious, too.

Joe asked, "What are you guys talking about?"

The next morning, she said, "Tell him." I laughed and said, "Sweetie, you have to have sex to get pregnant, and we have not been alone. Besides, I am going through the change of life, and I can no longer have children."

We all laughed.

Janiece's Life Lessons

- ➢ Be open to step through the fear.

- ➢ Accept gifts from people, enjoy and appreciate that you are loved.

- ➢ Have fun with your children.

CHAPTER 23

Learning to Ride a Motorcycle (In My Mid-50s!)

> "Have the courage to begin, whatever you have been afraid to do."
> ~ Janiece Rendon

My husband loves to ride motorcycles. It was either him and his daughter or him and me riding on the motorcycle.

I told him, "You know if I learn how to ride a motorcycle we could ride as a family." I don't know what I was thinking. Off to motorcycle school I went. It was a cold morning, in the midst of fall, when I started my three-day motorcycle class in Northglenn, Colorado. I got there early. I was nervous and scared. I watched to see what type of people would be in class. I was hoping for some girls and yes, there were two other girls. We began by getting to know each other then telling the class why we were there.

Our instructor was a professional motorcycle rider. He opened up the school because he believed in safety on the bike. We watched videos, then we went out to the bikes. They had a variety of bikes. He showed us how to check our bikes before every ride to make sure the bikes were safe for each ride. We got on the bikes, and walked them back and forth with our legs. Then, we started the engines and began slowly riding.

I kept thinking to myself what the heck am I doing? I was fifty something, and I could barely ride a bicycle. (Of course, my husband told me not to tell them that part.) I did not know how to drive a stick shift in a car, and now I had to do it on a bike, and balance? Oh, was I in trouble.

I made it through the first day. Yippee! They brought us back in the classroom and told us to make sure we took Ibuprofen and drank lots of water. We were going to be sore because we used muscles that we normally did not use. Well, I followed the rules. As soon as I got home, I took my ibuprofen and drank tons of water.

When I woke up the next morning, I felt like I had been hit by a bus. I was very sore. I took some more ibuprofen and off to day two. We arrived at 7:00 am in the morning when the sun was barely coming up. It was cold outside. One of the girls had come the first day with her friend, a guy. I asked her where her friend was, and she said that he had not taken ibuprofen and he was so sore he could not get up that morning.

I thought to myself, he was a huge guy and he did not make it on the second day? I was doing good.

We did not spend much time in the classroom. Out to the bikes we go… Urg…

Day 2 was harder than day one. As I looked around, everyone was excited and wanted to be on the bike. I, on the other hand, wanted to go back to the classroom. The exercises got harder and harder. We made circles and figure eights, and followed each other closely so there was no room for procrastinating. I did not know how to manage the clutch so I kept dying out. The instructor told me at this point in the game that I should not be dying out. I really struggled with the clutch.

Every part of my limbs had to do something: my left hand worked the clutch, my right hand worked the throttle and front brake, my left foot worked the gears, and my right foot worked the rear brake. Then, they expected me to look at the speedometer and watch where I was going. Are you kidding me?

The instructor would say, "Where you look, the motorcycle goes." We were doing our figure eights, when my bike began heading toward the fence, and I was going fast. I yelled for help!

However, I knew in my heart that I was the only person who was going to help in this situation. Then I remembered the rule, where your eyes focus the bike will follow. I was focusing on crashing into that fence and my bike was following my eyes. I turned my head to the right and got myself back on track.

> "The same is true in life. Where we focus our attention, our life follows." ~ **Janiece Rendon**

Each time we went in new figure eights, the lanes narrowed to do tighter turns. I am telling you, I was scared and wanted to quit. I realized I had never learned how to trust the curves in life. I never stepped out of my comfort zone. I stayed in the safety zone in life and limited my potential. The bike taught me a lot about life. That is the reason I named my business, "Trust the Curves."

We will all have curves in life. Our roads will never be straight. If we learn how to trust the curve and lean with it, eventually, we will land ourselves on the straight road.

I thought about how much my husband loved to ride and it kept me going. Finally, day two was over. We got back in the classroom, took some more quizzes, and watched more safety videos (more like watching crash videos). The instructor really focused on safety. I know that was good, however, I was already scared and watching these videos did not help my fear of riding a motorcycle. Again, drink more water, take ibuprofen, and see you tomorrow.

* * * * *

Day 3 was the day we passed or failed. We began in the morning doing figure eights, and they began getting tighter and tighter. The tension was getting real. I could feel the pressure and it became more work than fun. I stopped too soon and down I went. I fell while coming to a stop. I could feel myself in slow motion falling down. My head hit the pavement and boom I was down. I jumped up, excited, and ready to get back on the bike. I had broken off the tip of the clutch. The instructor came running to make sure I was okay. I said I was fine. I was so excited, I fell, and survived. I was terrified of falling, but now that I had, I had mastered the fall.

He gave me the clutch part as a memory. I got back on the bike, and we rode some more. I had been riding tense for three days and my body was sore. I was not having fun, and I thought to myself, what I was doing there? I pulled out of line, took my bike to the front, and said that I was done. I was crying because I felt like a failure, but I was not there to work. I was there to have fun, and fun was not happening.

One of the girls said, "Do not leave. I know I am not going to pass either." I told her I was sorry but I needed to leave. I came to have fun and I was so tense every muscle hurt.

As I walked out of the area, I looked back and waved goodbye. I felt defeated and sad that I left, but there was too much pressure. People were behind you, and in front of you, and there was not room for mistakes. If you messed up the people behind you could fall. And the pressure was just too much.

Kind of like being micromanaged at work. At work, the pressure was so strong to be perfect in a job that I was not good at, that I made more mistakes. Not knowing I could say hold on, let me step back and ask for help, I kept going under pressure and went out on a five-month depression. Wow, this motorcycle school was a powerful life's lesson. Yes, I felt defeated, but I knew I was in control and would do it at my own pace. I went to my mother's grave and cried for what seemed like an eternity. I got up and went home.

Janiece's Life Lessons

- When you are not having fun in life; it is time for a change.

- Learn how to master your falls; just because you fall does not mean it is over.

- It is okay to stop, take a breath, then, do it on your own terms.

- In life, you need room to fall; give yourself the space to fall.

- Learn to speak up for yourself; trust your gut.

- It is important to inspect your vehicle before you go for a drive. Are the tires full? Do you have enough gas? Do you need windshield wipers? Etc. Prepare for a safe drive.

- Follow the rules of life; it could save you from pain.

- It is important to know the direction you are going in life; your life will follow your vision.

- Trust the curves in life; lean into the curves, for the curves are only temporary.

- Believe the straight road is ahead.

CHAPTER 24

Ask for What You Want

> "Trust the curves in life, God will lead you through, the ride is amazing."
>
> ~ Janiece Rendon

I asked Joe if we could buy a motorcycle. I was excited to learn at my own pace. He said, "Yes," and off we went shopping.

The instructor had said, when riding a motorcycle not all bikes are the same. It is like fitting your hand in a glove. When looking for a bike, I understood what he was trying to say. So true, not every bike I tried out felt right. I found it. I found the bike that was meant for me. It was a silver Honda Shadow 650 and it felt perfect.

My husband drove it home and I was now the proud owner of a motorcycle. We lived four blocks away from the Division of Motor Vehicle, so I went and got my motorcycle permit. I could ride down the alley, onto the street, turn left, and I was in their parking lot. My husband followed me on his huge 1800 bike. I felt safe because he was following me. I rode around and around the parking lot. After I got my courage up, I began following the pattern in the parking lot. I stopped and started until I got used to the clutch. I was getting better and the motorcycle did not die out. We did this every time it was nice outside. Because it was fall, we did not have too many days to ride. Winter set in and I was not able to ride. The motorcycle was parked until spring.

Spring arrived and my husband said, "Let's go for a ride." It had been so long I forgot how to ride. We started up the engines and checked our bikes. We put on our gear: helmet, jeans, gloves, boots, and long sleeve shirt. Then we pulled out to the alley. I had forgotten where the kickstand was. My bike kind of fell towards my husband's bike. I looked up at him, and I knew I was in trouble. He said some words that I will not repeat. He then said, "What the heck were you thinking?"

I said, "I forgot where the kickstand was." Not a good way to begin a motorcycle ride.

First day on the bike after a long winter. I asked him questions like: is this the clutch, and this is, etc.? We rode down the alley to the motor vehicle parking lot. The night before I took my motorcycle class, my husband wanted me to be comfortable on the bike. He let me walk his bike down the alley. Where he started it, and slowly he asked me to pick up my feet and glide. I am telling you the alley seemed so narrow. The dumpster and the opposite side of the fence seemed so close, like I could barely go through the alley. Now the alley was normal size, I had so much room.

We got to the parking lot, and I kept dying out on the bike. I got it under control and began riding, doing circles and figure eights. My husband waved me over to him.

I pulled up beside him and he said, "You need to take it out of first gear." Ah, I was enjoying going round and round. I began practicing with the gears going from first to second. I was feeling scared and almost threw myself off the bike. It was not a good motorcycle day.

I pulled up beside him and said like a little kid, "Can I be done now?"

He said, "I will take you home and come back for your bike."

I said, "I could ride four blocks."

He said, "you better take it out of first gear and go at least 25 miles an hour".

I did and was glad to be home, off the bike.

I had some good motorcycle days that followed. I was doing pretty well; I eventually rode to the park and around it. Oh, I drove around the block and rode to the mailbox while my daughter followed me on her bicycle.

Then, I told my husband, "Motorcycles are meant to ride and my bike sits more than is ridden. I know I am never going to ride on the main streets and will never ride on the highway. I want to sell the bike."

I was afraid he would be mad at me, but he was relieved. He said, "I am very proud of you for trying. However, your fear could get you hurt."

I said, "I know and I do not want to cause an accident."

We sold the bike to a woman who was ready to move up to the next level. She rode off into the sunset and my bike was now doing what it was supposed to do, go riding.

I felt a bit defeated and sad. However, riding a motorcycle is dangerous, and you need to have the confidence in yourself. I was very proud of myself for following through and giving it my best. Learning how to ride a motorcycle taught me how to ride life. If something were to happen while my husband and I were riding, I could jump on the bike to go get help. In addition, I now felt more comfortable riding with my husband. The great news is I do not have to do all the work. I can sit in the back and take pictures with my camera. Life is good.

I realized, in life I never took chances. I always played it safe. I never stepped out of my comfort zone. I let life happen instead of being the director of my life. I was now going to be in charge and help others learn how to trust the curves in their life. I felt so empowered to begin my new journey in life. Was I a failure because I chose to give up my motorcycle and not continue to ride? No, I am a success because I gave it my best. I learned so much about myself in the process and now I get to share my experience of life with others.

Janiece's Life Lessons

- ➢ In learning a new skill, it is important to learn at your own pace.

- ➢ Build up your courage; then begin stretching yourself.

- ➢ Be sure to wear the proper equipment.

- ➢ It is okay to stop if you are not feeling it. You can continue another time.

- ➢ Know when it is time to quit.

- ➢ Learn something from your experiences.

- ➢ Continue your journey to completion; it is a fantastic experience.

- ➢ Do not let anyone dictate your future with their words.

- ➢ You have the power to create your life; continue your journey.

EPILOGUE

I've taken a second shot at becoming an entrepreneur. I am the proud Founder of Trust the Curves, a speaking, training and consulting business, since 2013. It all started from my motorcycle experience. I am in the game. I have a great coach and some awesome mentors supporting me. I have successful people who believe in me and want me to succeed. I made the choice to graduate from corporate two days after my 55th birthday. I chose to take control of my life's direction.

No more layoffs. I get to control the handlebars of life. I am learning to trust the curves and follow my dreams. I may not be the next Zig Ziglar, but I can be the best Janiece Rendon. I have a story of hope, success, and the journey of fulfilling a passion. With this mix of ingredients, I can make the cake and share it with others.

Attitude, Attitude, Attitude is the key ingredient; it is a Choice you make to let go; be happy, and choose your destiny. Finally, you have to Trust the Curves in Life…then, Step into your Uniqueness.

If I can inspire at least one person in your audience, everyone wins. Let me help someone get on the road of life and follow, his or her passion.

I graduated with a Bachelor of Science degree in Business Administration and Human Resource Management, in 2008. I also received a certificate in Business Leadership and a certificate in Practical Psychology. Not too bad for someone who was told she could not read or write. I never would have believed that I would hold a dual Master's degree in Communication and Psychology.

If I can graduate from college, anything is possible. I believe you can also follow your dreams and make the impossible, possible. Do not let anyone dictate what you can and cannot do. You have the power to create your life. I was going to be the next Zig Ziglar, remember? I may not be the next Zig Ziglar yet, but that possibility is what carried me through all the layoffs and all the curves I experienced during my career. I'm not finished yet.

My mother was so proud of me. She told me when I graduated from college that she was going to take me to Hawaii. However, my mother died in March 2007 and was not able fulfill her promise. Perhaps one day I will get the honor to speak in Hawaii and cherish the experience.

Set your intention and our dream will happen.

Sincerely,
Janiece Rendon

TRUST THE Curves

Through perseverance, determination, and love, Janiece Rendon has from being a 34-year old woman without a high school diploma to the successful woman with a dual Master's degree in Communication and Psychology; a Graduate level certificate in Career/Life Coach; as well as, a Graduate level certificate in Organizational Training and Development. She is an Adjunct Professor of Public Speaking at Colorado Heights University.

Hire Janiece for
Your Next Big Event
Laugh. Think. Be Inspired.

♦ **The F.A.C.T.S. of Life**

The Keys to Success: Forgiveness, Attitude, Choice, Trust, and Step into Your Greatness. Janiece's unique storytelling ability will keep your audience engaged and asking for more.

- ♦ Women's Organizations ♦ Businesses
- ♦ Churches ♦ Universities and High Schools

janiece.rendon@gmail.com
♦ 303-589-5994 ♦
www.TrustTheCurves.com

www.ingramcontent.com/pod-product-compliance
Lightning Source LLC
Chambersburg PA
CBHW031137090426
42738CB00008B/1127